History

A Teacher's Resource Book of Photocopiable Worksheets

Sue Neale

Contents

Teacher's notes

Introduction

Using Information Technology in History is a resource book of photocopiable history activities which can be completed with the help of a computer. The activities cover a range of history topics at Key Stage 2 and provide challenging, yet readily accessible opportunities for pupils to develop their Information Technology (IT) skills, whilst developing their knowledge and understanding of history. All the activities are aimed primarily at Key Stage 2 pupils.

Organisation

It is expected that as history topics are taught, teachers will select worksheets to use that will support the ongoing work. For example, when teaching about the Tudors, teachers may wish to use the worksheet 'Cutting and pasting the Tudors', in which pupils are asked to cut and paste events that occurred during the Tudor period so that they appear in the correct chronological order. The worksheets have not been ordered or grouped in any particular way and should be seen as a flexible resource which can be dipped into as required.

Some of the activities can be completed by pupils working on their own but the majority will benefit pupils who work with a partner. By working in collaboration with others, pupils can discuss and refine their ideas further. Additionally, by approaching the activities in a shared way, pupils learn to co-operate with each other. Care should be taken, however, to ensure that one pupil doesn't dominate the activity to the detriment of the other. The importance of the role of helper should be emphasised to pupils, in addition to the importance of hands-on work, when introducing activities.

Each activity will need to be explained as it is introduced so that pupils are clear about what is expected of them. It is often advantageous to allow pupils who are more confident with the computer to attempt an activity first. These pupils can then help the subsequent pupils, who can then in turn help others. This chain effect of pupils helping each other is often beneficial, as it frees the teacher to concentrate on teaching the rest of the class.

Software

The activities included in this booklet do not specify the software required to complete them. It is expected that a range of software packages will be used. The following types of programs will be required, however: a database program, a spreadsheet program, a word processing program, a desk-top publishing program, a drawing program and a screen turtle program. Additionally, CD-ROMs will be needed. Explanations outlining the main function of each type of program can be found below.

CD-ROMs

A CD-ROM can store an immense amount of information. CD-ROMs can store text, pictures, photographs, sound and videos. There are many CD-ROMs available today. Many are used as reference tools and can be used in similar ways to a book. Pupils can search for information by using key words or topics.

A number of the activities in this book require the use of CD-ROMs. They can be completed using either CD-ROM encyclopaedias or history based CD-ROMs. Examples of popular history CD-ROMs which are used at Key Stage 2 include: Anglia's 'Ancient Egyptians', Dorling Kindersley's 'History of the World' and Microsoft's 'Ancient Lands'.

Pupils should be encouraged to handle CD-ROMs with care as they are sensitive to dirt, grease and scratches. The data on a CD-ROM is recorded on the underside of the disc (shiny side), so this part of the disc should not be touched at all, otherwise read errors may occur. The disc should be held by the edge when picked up. When not in use CD-ROMs should be stored in their original cases.

Database programs

A database program allows the user to store data in a structured way. The information in a database can be searched and sorted so that specific data can be located quickly and efficiently. Databases are usually used to store, present and retrieve information.

In the databases used in these materials, data is entered under headings called 'fields'. A database entitled 'Monarchs' might include the field headings: name, born, died, married and reigned. There are three types of field structure: alphabetic fields, numeric fields and alphanumeric fields. Alphabetic fields recognise letters, numeric fields recognise numbers and alphanumeric fields recognise both. When setting up fields, the type of field will normally need to be identified. Once the fields have been established, data can be entered. Each 'page' of information entered is called a 'record'.

a record

name:	Queen Victoria
born:	1819
died:	1901
married:	Prince Albert
reigned:	64 years

Once information has been stored in a database, records can be sorted and searched. Fields can be sorted numerically into ascending or descending order or alphabetically. Additionally, records can be sorted over, below or between a certain range. Specific information can be searched for. For example, after entering information into a database called 'Monarchs', a question that might be asked is 'who married Prince Albert?' Searches for information can also be made using more than one criterion.

Information that has been entered into a database can be printed out record by record or in sorted lists. Many programs also allow the information to be presented pictorially, as bar charts or pie charts, for example.

Databases can be incorporated into the history curriculum in a number of ways. Some database projects have been suggested in this booklet, but ideas for further activities will often emerge during the course of a topic. For example, when studying the Victorians, it may be that a visit to a local graveyard stimulates the idea for a grave stone database.

Two examples of primary school database programs are Black Cat's 'Clipboard' and Research Machine's 'Information Workshop'.

Spreadsheets

A spreadsheet is a type of program which allows data to be stored and manipulated. The spreadsheet looks like a grid and is made up of rows and columns. Each individual position on a spreadsheet is called a cell. A cell can be identified by selecting the column it is in and the row it is in. The columns are located by letters, the rows by numbers. For example, cell B2 is highlighted below:

	A	B	C	D
1				
2		B2		
3				

Numbers can be entered into cells. Calculations can take place on those numbers by inserting formulae. After entering formulae, calculations are automatically performed. For example, when multiplying the number 6 in cell A1, by the number 3 in cell B1, a formula could be inserted in cell C1. After entering the formula the answer will automatically appear in cell C1. An example of a formula in this case is =A1*B1. (Computers use * as the multiplication sign).

	A	B	C
1	6	3	=A1*B1
2			
3			

Teachers will need to refer to the software manuals of the spreadsheet package they are using for details of formulae that can be used with a particular program.

Text can also be entered on to a spreadsheet. This usually helps explain what the numbers mean. Sometimes, when inserting text, the columns will need to be widened. This is usually done by moving the cursor to the top of the column and dragging with the mouse.

Spreadsheets can be used to present a wide variety of information. The real value of using a spreadsheet, however, is that once a spreadsheet has been completed, should any changes be made to numeric values or formulae, the effects of the changes upon the rest of the spreadsheet are immediately displayed. An example of a popular primary spreadsheet package is Research Machine's 'Starting Grid' which is a package built around Microsoft Excel.

A variety of graphs can be constructed by using the graphics facility of a spreadsheet. A bar chart, pie chart or line graph is usually constructed by entering columns of data on to a spreadsheet grid, highlighting them and then clicking on a chart tool button, icon or word.

Word processing

Word processing involves entering text via a keyboard, using a word processing program. A range of word processing programs is available today, for use in schools. Word processing is popular as it makes writing an easier and less frustrating activity. Pupils who usually find writing a chore are often motivated by the impressive results which they can achieve by using a word processor.

The appearance of text can be changed when using a word processor. It can be enlarged or reduced in size, and the style and colour can also be altered to give interesting results.

The following activities require the teacher to enter text and save it prior to pupils beginning the activity: Cutting and pasting the Tudors and Gods and Goddesses.

Desk-top publishing

Desk-top publishing programs are particularly good to use when producing newspapers, newsletters and advertisements. They are good because they allow pictures and text to be inserted into boxes (frames). These boxes can then be moved around. Additionally, the boxes can be made bigger or smaller and given borders. An example of a popular desk-top publishing program is Microsoft's 'Publisher'.

Drawing programs

There are a number of programs that allow the user to draw and design pictures. Images can usually be drawn freely using different brush types or straight lines can be created with a variety of line thicknesses. Colours are usually selected from a palette. Some programs allow the user to stamp on a selection of ready drawn pictures without leaving the program.

Screen turtles

A screen turtle is a cursor that can be commanded to move around the screen. By typing in commands, the turtle can be made to draw lines, a picture or a pattern. Using a screen turtle involves the use of angles, estimating distances and the sequencing and modification of commands. 'Logo' is a popular computer language which uses a screen turtle.

The Minotaurs's maze worksheet requires pupils to command a screen turtle through a maze. This maze will need to be photocopied on to an acetate worksheet prior to the pupils beginning the activity.

Assessment

The activities in this book require pupils to provide either written or printed evidence of their work. It is a good idea for pupils to have a folder in which to store this work. A pupil's record sheet is provided which can be copied and completed by each child, for each activity. In addition to examining recorded evidence of pupils' work, teachers should observe pupils working at a computer, in order to assess their levels of confidence.

Printing

Children should be taught to use printing resources carefully. Pupils should 'print preview' their work where possible, prior to printing. They should only be encouraged to print, when they have completed an activity. Almost all of the activities which require the use of a printer can be completed using a black and white printer. A colour printer may give more impressive results for some of the activities, however.

National Curriculum

The National Curriculum for IT at Key Stage 2 states that IT should be used to explore and solve problems in the context of work across a variety of subjects, including history. Additionally, the National Curriculum for History at Key Stage 2 outlines certain requirements for the use of Information Technology. For example, it is stated that pupils should be given opportunities where appropriate to develop their information technology capability in their study of history. By providing worksheets that satisfy a significant proportion of the IT and History Programmes of Study at Key Stage 2 it is hoped that teachers will find it easier to deliver curriculum requirements.

The activities in this booklet relate to the following Statements of Attainment:

IT Key Stage 2 Programme of Study
1a, 1b, 1c.
Communicating and handling information: 2a, 2b, 2c, 2d.
Controlling, monitoring and modelling: 3a, 3c.

History Key Stage 2 Programme of Study
Key Elements: 1a, 1b, 2a, 4a, 4b, 5a, 5b, 5c.
Study Unit 1: Romans, Anglo-Saxons, and Vikings in Britain: 2a, 2b, 2c.
Study Unit 2: Life in Tudor Times a, e.
Study Unit 3a: Victorian Britain: c.
Study Unit 3b: Britain Since 1930: a, b, c, e.
Study Unit 4: Ancient Greece: c, e.
Study Unit 5: Local History: a.
Study Unit 6: A past non European society: a, b.

The specific IT skills that are used within each worksheet, are identified in the table on the next page.

Glossary

CD-ROM (Compact Disc Read-Only Memory) A compact disc which can store a huge amount of data.
Cell A cell is a box found on a spreadsheet grid. A cell is located by its column letter and row number. Information can be entered into cells in the form of text or numbers.
Clip art Ready drawn images that can be incorporated in a piece of work or printed out separately.
Cut and Paste A facility that allows data to be moved from one place to another.
Data Information that is entered into or produced by a computer. The data may be in the form of numbers, text, graphics or sounds.
Database An organised store of information.
Field A heading used on a record in a database.
Font A particular style and size of typeface.
Formulae Mathematical equations which can be used in a spreadsheet to carry out equations.
Print Preview A facility which allows the layout of a document to be checked prior to printing.
Record A 'page' of information entered into a database program.
Screen Turtle A screen cursor which can be programmed to move in response to commands.
Software Programs for a computer.
Spelling Checker A facility offered by word processors which allows you to check spellings.
Spreadsheet A grid of cells. Data can be entered into these cells and then calculations performed on that data by using formulae.
Word Processing A term used to describe the process of entering, storing and revising text.

Information Technology Skills – a checklist

	Anglo-Saxon house	Come to the public baths!	Henry VIII	Second World War artefacts	Famous Victorians	Minotaur's maze	Cutting and pasting the Tudors	Olympic rings	Monarch search	Food rationing	Questionnaire of the decade	Finding out about the Vikings	Aztec pictograms	Britain is at war!	Local sources	Ancient Egypt	Save and salvage	Tudor monarchs	True or false?	Tudor menu	Gods and goddesses	Aztec temple	Queen Victoria's time	Project cover
load work							■								■						■			
save work		■	■	■			■	■		■	■		■	■	■		■	■		■	■			■
print preview		■	■				■	■			■		■	■			■	■		■	■			■
print		■	■	■			■	■			■		■	■	■		■	■		■	■			■
edit text		■	■				■				■			■			■			■	■			■
use spelling checker			■								■			■										
collect date				■											■									
set up database				■											■									
search database															■								■	
sort database															■									
change size of font		■												■			■			■				■
change style of font		■												■			■			■				■
underline text																		■		■				■
cut and paste							■																	
create spreadsheet										■														
insert formulae										■														
search CD-ROM	■		■		■				■			■				■		■	■			■	■	
insert clipart/picture		■	■														■			■				■
command a screen turtle						■																		
create text frame														■										
process information			■	■			■			■	■			■	■			■			■			
retrieve information	■		■		■				■	■		■			■	■		■	■			■	■	
solve problems using IT					■	■	■		■	■		■				■		■	■		■		■	
produce table																		■						
draw image		■						■					■				■			■				■

Name ....

Anglo- Saxon house

Find a picture of an Anglo-Saxon house on a CD-ROM.
Sketch the house in the box below.

Answer the questions below about the house you have sketched.

1 What is the roof made of ? ....

2 What are the walls made of ? ....

3 How many rooms are there ? ....

4 Explain how the house is heated. ....
....

5 Describe the windows and doors. ....
....

Name ....

Come to the public baths!

The Romans enjoyed going to the baths. They went to get clean but they also went to meet friends, play games, gamble and chat. Often people would have a massage or go for a swim.

A typical Roman bath would include a hot room, a steam room, a warm room, a cold room, an exercise area and a gaming area. Some baths had restaurants or libraries.

Produce an A4 - sized poster to attract people to the baths.

Useful Tips

- Plan your work on a piece of paper before you begin at the computer. Your completed poster should fill one side of an A4 sheet only.
- Consider how you are going to align the text. Most posters are 'centre aligned'.
- Select a style of font that will give extra effect to your poster.
- Make the text large enough so that it can be seen clearly but don't keep all of the text the same size.
- Paste a picture on to your poster.
- Save your work on a regular basis.
- Print preview your work prior to printing.

Print out your finished poster.

Name ....

3 Henry VIII

Henry VIII was a Tudor *monarch*. A *monarch* is a king or queen. Monarchs were very powerful during Tudor times.

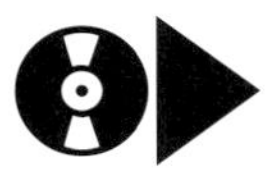

Henry VIII led an interesting life. Find out about his life using a CD-ROM. Make notes on a piece of paper using the key words below to help you carry out your research.

height

born

wives

mother

personality

father

hair

eyes

home

education

crowned

died

After you have collected enough information, word process an account of his life.

Save your work and then print out a copy of the text to show to your teacher. After your teacher has seen your work, make any changes necessary.

Try to find a clipart or CD-ROM picture of Henry VIII and paste it into your work.

Print out your completed account.

4

Name ....

Second World War artefacts

We can find out more about a period in history by examining artefacts. An artefact is something that has been made.

The artefacts shown below are all from the Second World War. Write down what you think they are.

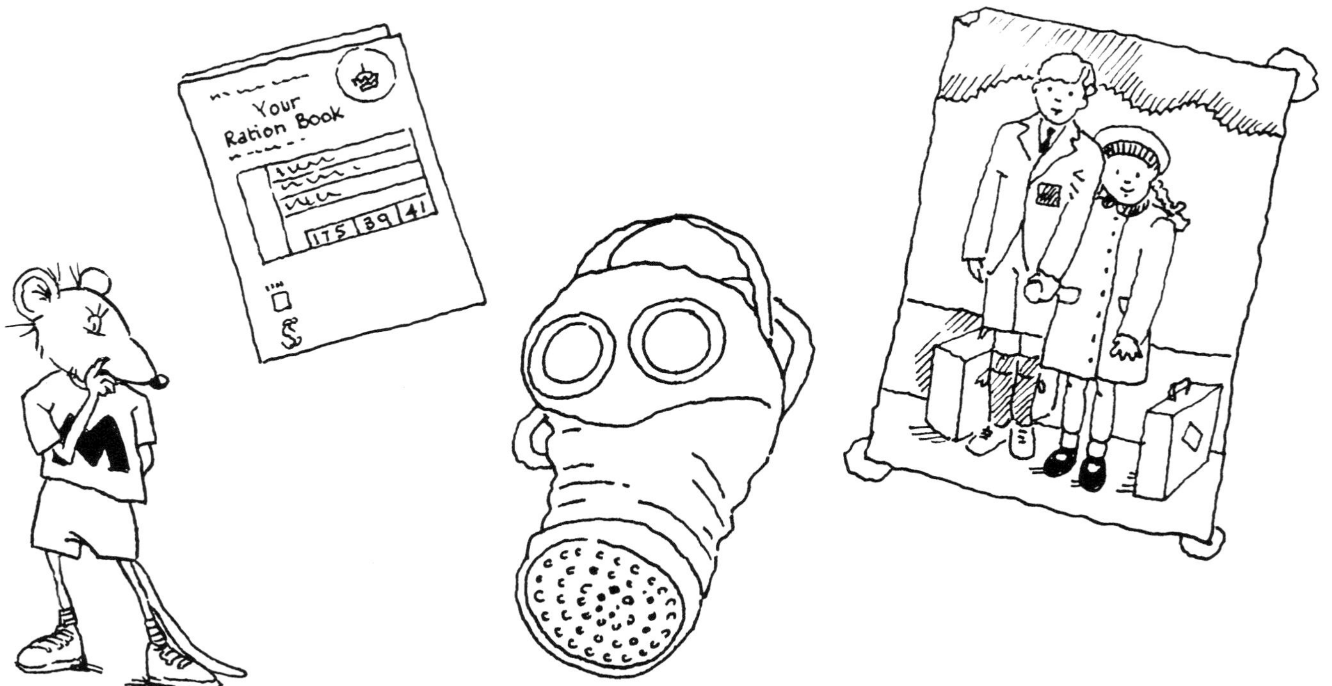

With your class, make a collection of artefacts from the Second World War.

Store information about the artefacts in a database. Use these field headings: **description**, **year** and **owner**.

As each item is brought into school, add the information about it to your database.

description: gas mask

date: 1941

owner: Mr Bloggs

Sort out the records into alphabetical order and then print out each record.

Display the data you have printed out next to the artefacts to create an interesting classroom display.

Name ....

5 Famous Victorians

There were many Victorians who became famous.
Use a CD-ROM to find out what the Victorians below were famous for.

Complete the chart.

Victorian	Famous for
Florence Nightingale	
David Livingstone	
Charles Dickens	
Isambard Kingdom Brunel	
George Stephenson	
Mary Kingsley	

Can you find the names of any more famous Victorians?
Write down their names below.

....

....

Name ....

The Minotaur's maze

Note to teacher: the next page should be photocopied on to acetate for this activity.

Read the story below about a Greek mythical monster called Minotaur.

The Minotaur lived on the island of Crete in a very large maze. The Minotaur was a strange creature. He had the head of a bull and the body of a man.

Every year the king of Crete ordered seven youths and seven maidens to go into the maze. They were never seen again and were either lost, starved to death or eaten by the Minotaur.

One year, Theseus offered to be one of the seven to go into the maze. The king's daughter loved him and decided to help him. She gave him a ball of string which she told him to unwind as he went in to the maze.

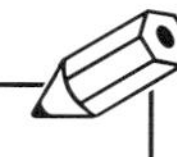

What do you think The Minotaur looked like? Draw a picture in this box.

Can you guide Theseus back to the king's daughter?

Load a program that allows you to control a screen turtle by typing in commands.

Place the acetate worksheet that accompanies this activity over your computer screen so that the screen turtle appears in the box where Theseus is.

Guide the turtle through the maze back to the king's daughter without going over the lines.

Name ....

The Minotaur's maze (continued)

Note to teacher: This page should be photocopied on to acetate for Activity 6.

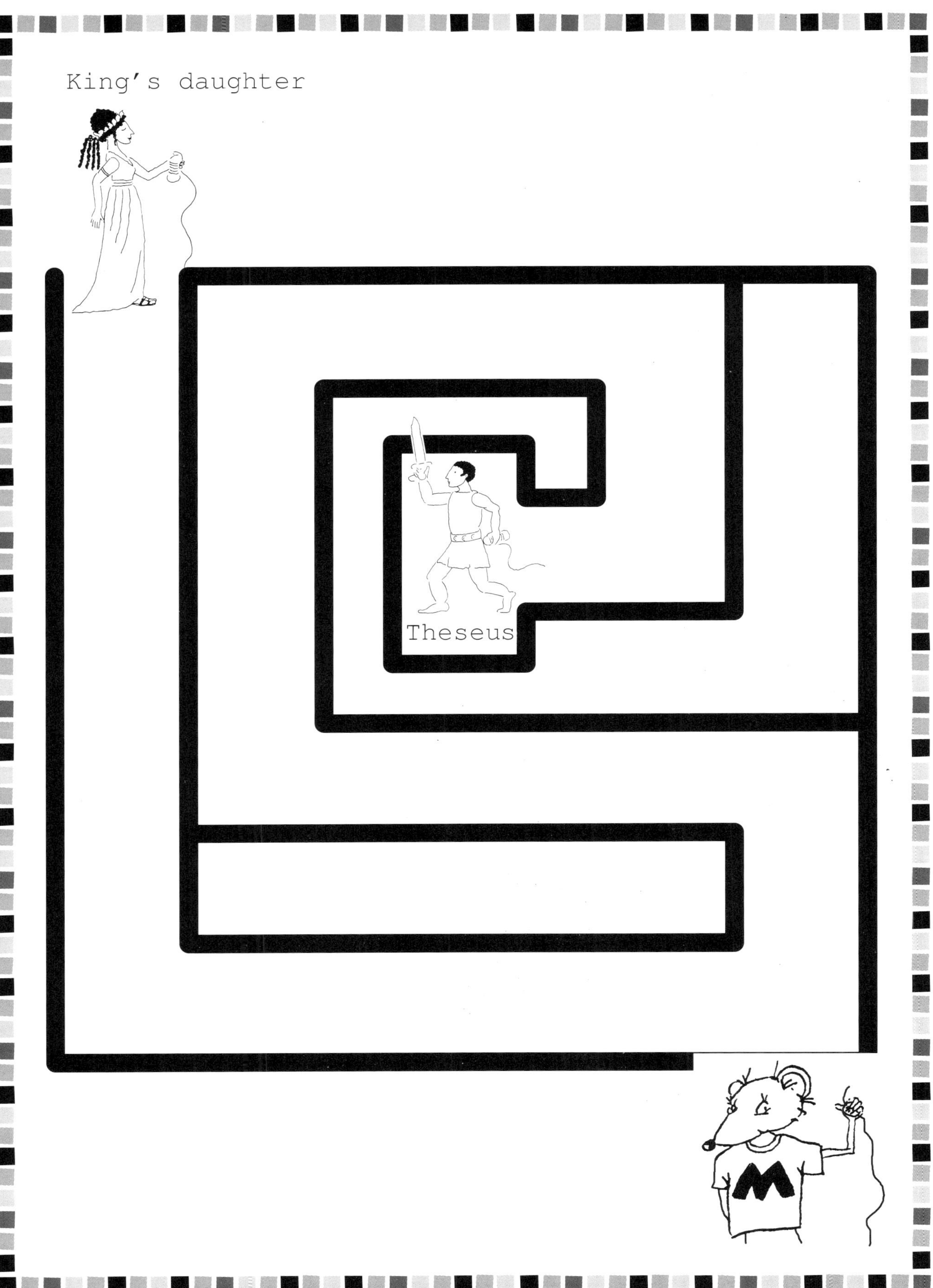

7

Name ....

Cutting and pasting the Tudors

In history, times and dates are important because they help us to put events in the past in the correct order. Putting events in the correct order is called *chronology*.

Below is a list of some important events that occurred during the Tudor period. Load this information on to your computer or type it in yourself.

Find out when the events occurred and write the dates on this sheet. Then on your computer cut and paste the information so that it appears in the correct order.

Henry VIII becomes king.	........▶	....
A fleet of ships called the Spanish Armada is sent by King Philip of Spain to invade England.	........▶	....
Edward VI becomes king.	........▶	....
Mary I becomes queen.	........▶	....
The Mary Rose sinks on her way to fight the French.	........▶	....
Elizabeth I becomes queen.	........▶	....
Henry VII becomes king.	........▶	....

Once you have pasted the events into the correct order, print out your work.

Name ....

Olympic rings

The ancient Greeks invented the Olympic Games. They were first held at a p.ace called Olympia in honour of the chief god, Zeus. Today the Olympic Games are held every 4 years.

The Olympic Games are recognisable by the symbol of five interlocking rings. The five rings represent five continents of the world.

Look at the Olympic rings below.

Use a drawing program to copy the Olympic symbol.

Print out your work.

Can you des gn a symbol for your school sports day ?

Print out your work.

Name ....

Monarch search

Use a database or a CD-ROM to search for the information needed to answer the questions below.

1 In which year did James II become king? ....

2 How many years was George V king for? ....

3 Which king plotted to blow up the Houses of Parliament? ....

4 Who did Mary I marry? ....

5 Who became queen in 1558? ....

6 Which monarch married Katherine of Aragon? ....

7 Who was the king before Elizabeth II? ....

8 How many years was James I king for? ....

9 In which year did Henry VIII become king? ....

10 Which monarch died in 1901? ....

11 When did Henry V1 die? ....

12 Who became King after Richard III? ....

13 When did Henry II begin his reign? ....

14 When did Mary I die? ....

15 How many years was Charles I king for? ....

10

Name ....

Food rationing

Food was rationed during the Second World War. A typical adult's food ration for one week was:

225g sugar, 50g butter, 100g margarine,
85g cheese, 85g cooking fat, 100g bacon,
50g jam, 50g tea, 60g sweets, 1.7 litres milk,
1s 2d's worth of meat and 1 egg.

cheese ration 1 gram

Copy the information below on to a spreadsheet.

Food	Total weight (g)	Ration for one adult (g)	Number of rations
sugar	0	225	
butter	0	50	
magarine	0	100	
cheese	0	85	
cooking fat	0	85	
bacon	0	100	
jam	0	50	
sweets	0	60	
tea	0	50	

Put formula here!

Use your spreadsheet to help you calculate the answers to the questions below. (You will need to insert formulae on to your spreadsheet to do this).

1 How many adults could receive their weekly ration from 680g of cooking fat? ....

2 A shopkeeper had a block of cheese which weighed 425g. How many customers could receive their ration of cheese? ....

3 A shopkeeper had a large bag of sugar which weighed 4725g. How many customers could receive their ration of sugar? ....

4 Which would serve more people: 1550g of tea or 1740g of sweets? ....

5 A shopkeeper had 5kg of each type of food. How many customers could he serve if each customer received their full weekly ration? ....

11

Name

Questionnaire of the decade

We can find out information about recent decades in history by asking people questions.

Write down 5 questions that you could ask someone in order to find out what life was like during one of the decades since 1930.

Here are some key words that may help you when designing questions.

fashion transport music inventions school food people entertainment homes

Questions

1 ....

....

2 ....

....

3 ....

....

4 ....

....

Word process your questions so that you end up with a well-presented questionnaire. Leave spaces for the person reading it to write in their answers.

Print out your completed question sheet.

12

Name ....

Finding out about the Vikings

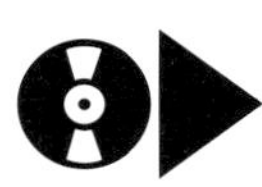

Use a CD-ROM to search for the information you need to answer the questions below .

1 Which three countries did the Vikings come from?

....

2 The Vikings gave names to places where they settled. What name did they give for a field? ....

3 The Vikings captured York in 866 AD. What name did they give York? ....

4 Who was the first Viking to become king of England? ....

5 What were the letters called that the Vikings used when writing? ....

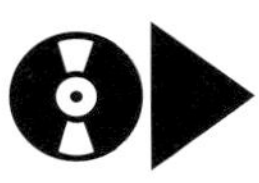

For 300 years the Vikings were the best ship-builders in Europe. Find a picture of a Viking ship on a CD-ROM and sketch it in the box below.

13

Name ....

Aztec pictograms

The Aztecs did not use letters to write with but instead they used pictograms. Pictograms are pictures that represent words.

What words do you think the pictograms below represent?

1 ....   2 ....   3 ....

Can you invent some of your own pictograms ?

Use a drawing program to design a pictogram to represent one of the following.

sun   *temple*   *book*   *snake*

Plan your design below before you begin at the computer.

Print out your completed design.

14

Name ....

Britain is at war!

Newspapers are excellent sources of information. Many newspapers were produced continually throughout the Second World War despite paper rationing and air raids.

Imagine that you are a journalist in 1939. The Prime Minister has just declared that Britain is at war with Germany.

You have been passed the information below.

On Sunday September 3rd 1939 at 11.15 am Mr Chamberlain spoke on the wireless.

It was a sunny day.

He said "I have to tell you that this country is now at war with Germany."

Mr Chamberlain's speech was followed by the playing of 'God Save the King'.

30 minutes later, air raid sirens could be heard in London.

Produce a newspaper report that could appear on the front page of the newspaper you are working for.

Give your article a catchy headline in large, bold print. Make up a subheading. A subheading usually summarises what the article is about. The letters in the subheading should be smaller than those in the headline but larger than those that make up the main body of the text. The main body of the text is usually written in columns.

Look at this example of a newspaper report showing a headline and a subheading.

Queen visits school

On Monday 6th May, the Queen met pupils and teachers at Parkfield Junior

The pupils and teachers cheered as her majesty

First she took a look around the new science

Print out your completed report.

Name ....

Local sources

When historians want to find out something about the past, they rely on sources. A source can be almost anything. For example, newspapers and books are sources.

Sources can be divided into two types:

and

Primary sources are sources that come from a particular period of study, whilst secondary sources are sources that give information about a period in history but have been produced at a later date.

Roman coin – Primary source

text book – secondary source

Find out about the history of your local area by collecting primary and secondary sources.

Keep a record of the sources you have collected by entering the information into a database using the field headings shown in the record below.

description: History of Pinner (book)

date: 1981

source: secondary

Keep adding to your database as more sources are collected.

At the end of your project sort out your data into two groups: *primary sources* and *secondary sources*.

Print out the data.

16

Name ....

Ancient Egypt

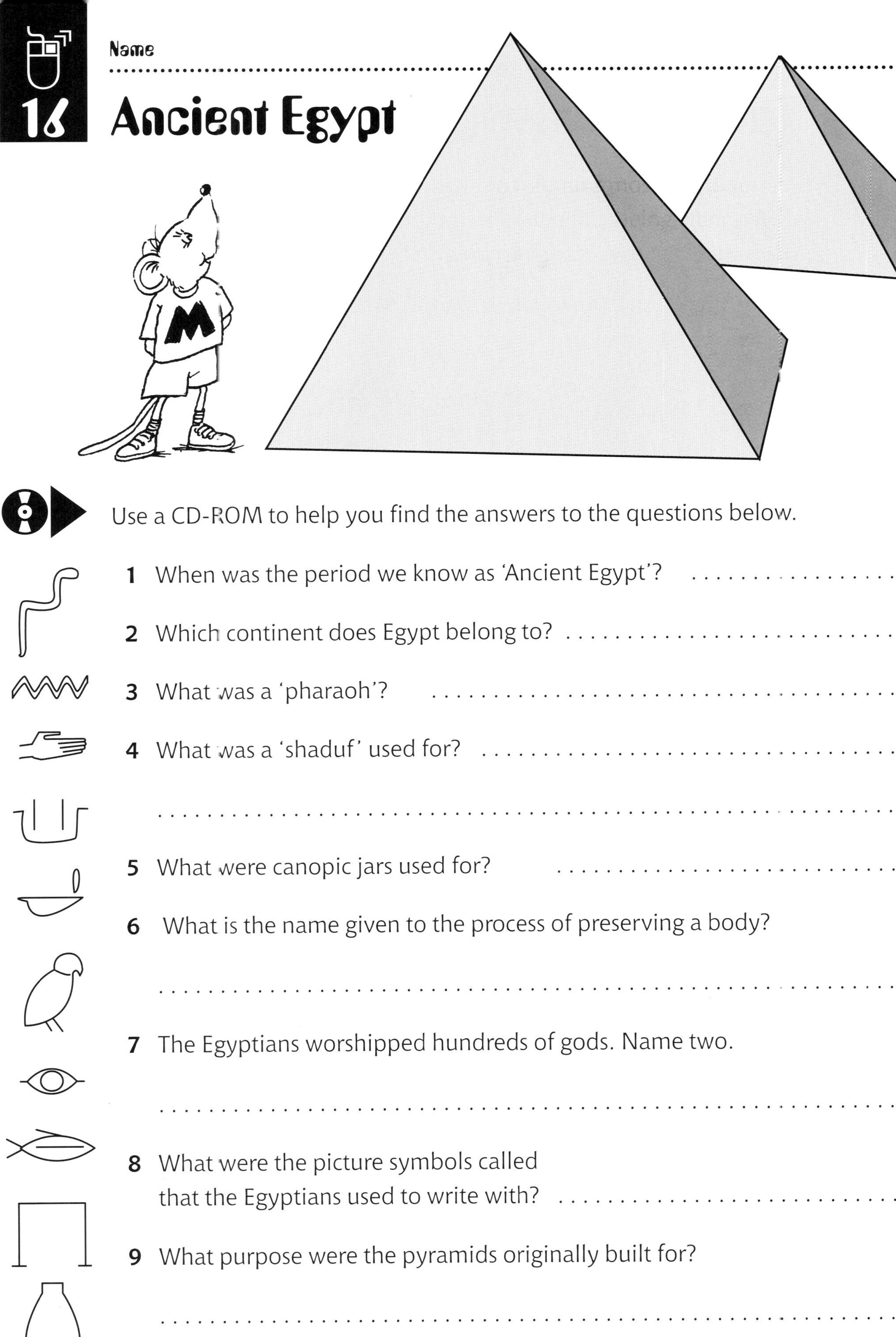

Use a CD-ROM to help you find the answers to the questions below.

1 When was the period we know as 'Ancient Egypt'? ....

2 Which continent does Egypt belong to? ....

3 What was a 'pharaoh'? ....

4 What was a 'shaduf' used for? ....

....

5 What were canopic jars used for? ....

6 What is the name given to the process of preserving a body?

....

7 The Egyptians worshipped hundreds of gods. Name two.

....

8 What were the picture symbols called that the Egyptians used to write with? ....

9 What purpose were the pyramids originally built for?

....

10 What is the name of the river that runs through Egypt which was very important to the ancient Egyptians? ....

Name ....

Save and salvage

During the Second World War, people were encouraged to save all items made of materials that were in short supply. These materials were then re-processed and used for the war effort.

Paper, old tins and clothes are three examples of materials that were 'salvaged'.

Posters and advertisements were produced to remind people to be more careful with resources.

What do you think this poster encouraged people to recycle ?

Design your own Second World War poster that would remind people to be more careful when using one of the following resources:

clothes *food* *paper* *metal*

It is often a good idea to create a slogan to catch the reader's eye. A slogan is really a catchy saying.

For example,

MAKE-DO AND MEND

was a slogan used in the war.

Print out your finished poster.

Name ....

Tudor monarchs

The Tudors were a powerful family who ruled for most of the sixteenth century. There were five Tudor monarchs, the first being Henry VII.

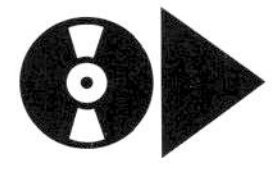

Use a CD-ROM to find the information you need to copy and complete the table below.

Tudor monarch	Year reign began	Year reign ended
Henry VII		
Henry VIII		
Edward VI		
Mary I		
Elizabeth I		

Underneath the table, write a sentence to say which Tudor ruled for the longest.

Print out your work.

Name ....

True or false?

Look carefully at the historical statements listed below.
Some of the statements are true and some are false.

Draw a circle around the words **true** or **false** to show whether you agree with the statement or disagree.

1	The Black Death was a deadly plague carried by fleas on mice.	**true**	**false**
2	The Great Fire of London began in 1666.	**true**	**false**
3	The telephone was invented in 1876 by John Logie Baird.	**true**	**false**
4	Winston Churchill was Prime Minister from 1940 to 1945.	**true**	**false**
5	The Second World War started in 1939 and finished in 1945.	**true**	**false**
6	Florence Nightingale nursed soldiers in the First World War.	**true**	**false**
7	The Domesday Book was completed in 1186.	**true**	**false**
8	The Battle of Britain between British and German air forces took place over England in 1940.	**true**	**false**
9	Queen Victoria became the Empress of India in 1874.	**true**	**false**
10	A primary source is an object found in a school.	**true**	**false**

Check to see if you were right by searching for the answers in a CD-ROM encyclopaedia.

How many did you get right ? Write down your score.

$\frac{\quad}{10}$

Name ....

Tudor menu

During Tudor times feasts and banquets were popular amongst the wealthy.

Many feasts and banquets would last all night. The main part of the meal was usually meat, such as deer, wild boar, lamb, poultry and beef. There were no refrigerators so meat was often salted or dried to preserve it.

Bread was often served with the meat. The food was usually washed down with beer, ale, cider or water.

Produce a menu that could be given at a Tudor meal.

Print out your completed menu.

21

Name ....

Gods and goddesses

The ancient Greeks had many different gods and goddesses.

Load the information that appears below on to your computer.

Cut and paste the text so that the appropriate descriptions match the correct god or goddess.

HERMES
ZEUS
ATHENA
APOLLO
HEPHAESTES
APHRODITE

He was the father to many other gods.
She was the goddess of wisdom and war.
He was the god of poetry, music, archery and healing.
She was the most beautiful goddess. She was the goddess of love.
He was the messenger of the gods.
He was the blacksmith god and the god of fire.

Print out your finished work.

22

Name ....

Aztec temple

The Aztecs ived over 500 years ago in the region that is now called Mexico.

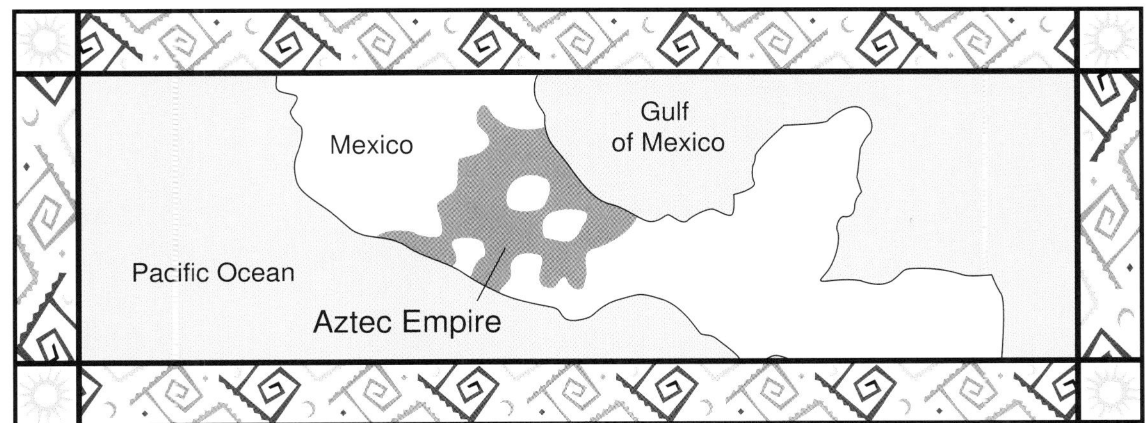

The Aztecs were powerful people. They built large pyramid temples for their gods. Ceremonies and sacrifices took place at the top of the temples.

Find a picture of an Aztec temple on a CD-ROM. Sketch the temple in the box below.

23

Name ....

Queen Victoria's time

Queen Victoria reigned for 64 years. This was longer than any other British monarch.

Use a CD-ROM or a database to search for the dates that match the different events in her life.

1 Queen Victoria died. ....▶ ....

2 Her son, Albert, became king. ....▶ ....

3 Queen Victoria married Prince Albert. ....▶ ....

4 Prince Albert died. ....▶ ....

5 Victoria became queen. ....▶ ....

6 Queen Victoria celebrated her Golden Jubilee. ....▶ ....

7 Victoria was born in Kensington Palace. ....▶ ....

8 Queen Victoria became the Empress of India. ....▶ ....

9 Queen Victoria celebrated her Diamond Jubilee. ....▶ ....

On a piece of paper draw your own timeline like the one below. Add the events to it so that they appear chronologically.

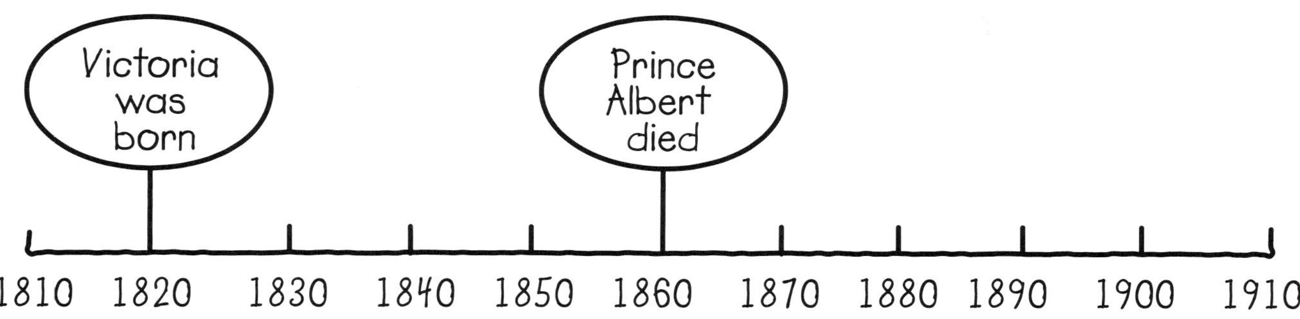

24

Name ....

Project cover

It is likely at some stage that your teacher will ask you to do your own research and produce a history project.

When producing a project, it is important that the information you have acquired is presented clearly, attractively and in an organised manner.

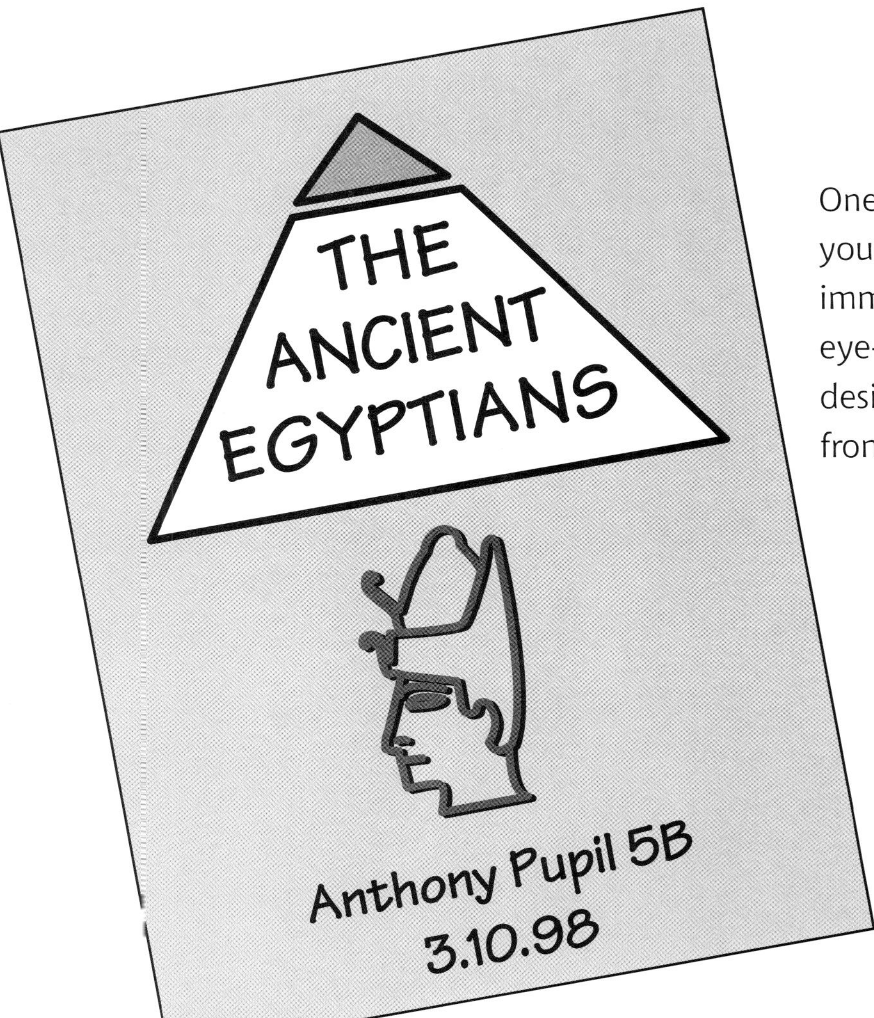

One way of making your project immediately more eye-catching is to design an interesting front cover design.

Design a project cover for a project you are working on.

You will need to ensure that you include the following information:

- the title of the project
- your name
- a date to show when the project was produced.

Plan out your design on a piece of paper before you begin at the computer.

Print out your finished work.

Name .... Date ....

Pupil's record sheet

Activity ....

Software used ....

What I did ....

....

....

....

....

....

What I learnt ....

....

....

....

....

....

I found this activity . . . *(circle appropriate words)*

hard **easy** **fun** **enjoyable** **frustrating**

boring **challenging** **interesting** **exciting**

Solutions and examples

2 Come to the public baths!

See example on page 32.

4 Second World War artefacts

Ration book, photograph and gas mask.

5 Famous Victorians

Florence Nightengale – nurse
David Livingstone – missionary and explorer
Charles Dickens – writer
Isambard Kingdom Brunel – engineer who designed steam ships and bridges
George Stevenson – railway engineer who built the first steam locomotive
Mary Kingsley – explorer

7 Cutting and pasting the Tudors

1. Henry VII becomes king
2. Henry VIII becomes king
3. The Mary Rose sinks on her way to fight the French
4. Edward VI becomes king
5. Mary I becomes queen
6. Elizabeth I becomes queen
7. A fleet of ships called the Spanish Armada is sent by King Philip of Spain to invade England

8 Olympic rings

See example on page 32

9 Monarch search

1. 1685
2. 26 years
3. James 1
4. Philip of Spain
5. Elizabeth 1
6. Henry VIII
7. George VI
8. 22 years
9. 1509
10. Queen Victoria
11. 1471
12. Henry VII
13. 1154
14. 1558
15. 24 years

10 Food rationing

1. 8 adults
2. 5 customers
3. 21 customers
4. 1550g tea
5. 22 customers

	A	B	C	D
1	**Food weight (g)**	**Total ration (g)**	**One adult ration**	**Number of rations**
2	sugar	0	225	**= B2/C2**
3	butter	0	50	**= B3/C3**
4	margerine	0	100	**= B4/C4**
5	cheese	0	85	**= B5/C5**
6	cooking fat	0	85	**= B6/C6**
7	bacon	0	100	**= B7/C7**
8	jam	0	50	**= B8/C8**
9	sweets	0	60	**= B9/C9**
10	tea	0	50	**= B10/C10**

12 Finding out about the Vikings

1. Denmark, Norway, Sweden
2. 'thwaite'
3. Jorvik
4. King Knut
5. Runes

13 Aztec pictograms

1. Volcano
2. alligator
3. rabbit

16 Ancient Egypt

1. approx. 3100BC – 30BC
2. Africa
3. an Egyptian King
4. to move water
5. to store internal organs in
6. embalming
7. the many gods include Bastet, Bes, Hapi, Anubis, Isis, Horus, Osiris and Thoth
8. hieroglyphs
9. to bury pharaohs in
10. The Nile

18 Tudor monarchs

Tudor monarch	Year reign began	Year reign ended
Henry VII	1485	1509
Henry VIII	1509	1547
Edward VI	1547	1553
Mary I	1553	1558
Elizabeth I	1558	1603

19 True or false?

1. **false** (the plague was carried by rats)
2. **true**
3. **true**
4. **true**
5. **true**
6. **false** (Florence Nightingale nursed soldiers in the Crimean war)
7. **false** (the Domesday book was completed in 1086)
8. **true**
9. **false** (Queen Victoria became the Empress of India in 1876)
10. **false** (A primary source is a source that has originated from the period in history that is being referred to.)

21 Gods and goddesses

Zeus He was the father to many other gods.
Athena She was the goddess of wisdom and war.
Apollo He was the god of poetry, music, archery and healing.
Aphrodite She was the most beautiful goddess. She was the goddess of love.
Hermes He was the messenger of the gods
Hephaestes He was the blacksmith god and the god of fire.

23 Queen Victoria's time

1 Queen Victoria died 1901
2 Albert became King 1901
3 Queen Victoria married Prince Albert 1840
4 Prince Albert died 1861
5 Victoria became Queen 1837
6 Queen Victoria celebrated her Golden Jubilee 1887
7 Victoria was born in Kensington Palace 1819
8 Queen Victoria became the Empress of India 1876
9 Queen Victoria celebrated her Diamond Jubilee 1897

8 Olympic Rings

2 Come to the public baths!

A2

Wilfried Krenn
Herbert Puchta

ARBEITSBUCH, Lektion 9–18
Deutsch als Fremdsprache

mit Audios online

Hueber Verlag

Die Online-Übungen, die Lösungen zu den Aufgaben im Arbeitsbuch, die Transkriptionen zu allen Hörtexten und weiteres Material finden Sie unter www.hueber.de/motive

▶ 103 Die Audios zum Arbeitsbuch finden Sie unter www.hueber.de/motive

3. 2. 1. | Die letzten Ziffern
2027 26 25 24 23 | bezeichnen Zahl und Jahr des Druckes.
Alle Drucke dieser Auflage können, da unverändert, nebeneinander benutzt werden.
1. Auflage

Umschlaggestaltung: Sieveking · Agentur für Kommunikation, München
Layout und Satz: Sieveking · Agentur für Kommunikation, München
Druck und Bindung: Westermann Druck Zwickau GmbH, Zwickau
Printed in Germany
ISBN 978-3-19-041881-7

Art. 530_30201_001_01

Vorwort

Liebe Lernende!

Das Arbeitsbuch zu MOTIVE soll Ihnen helfen, den Lernstoff des Kursbuches selbstständig zu vertiefen und zu üben. Die Aufgaben im Arbeitsbuch sind exakt auf das Kursbuch abgestimmt und greifen die Inhalte des Kursbuches wieder auf.

Aufbau einer Lektion im Arbeitsbuch

Lernwortschatz
Am Beginn jeder Arbeitsbuchlektion finden Sie den Lernwortschatz mit Angaben zum Sprachgebrauch in der Schweiz (CH) und in Österreich (A). Die Wortlisten sind nach den Übungsnummern des Kursbuches (A1, A2 usw.) geordnet.

A-Doppelseite, B-Doppelseite, C-Doppelseite
Jeder Doppelseite im Kursbuch entspricht genau eine Doppelseite im Arbeitsbuch. Die Übungschronologie des Arbeitsbuches folgt dem Kursbuch, sodass Sie schnell passende Aufgaben finden, um die Grammatik, den Wortschatz und die Redemittel aus dem Kursbuch zu üben. Ein Verweissystem unterstützt Sie dabei.

Die Lese- und Hörtexte des Kursbuches präsentieren den neuen Wortschatz und die neue Grammatik. Eine intensive Auseinandersetzung mit diesen Texten ist für Ihren Lernerfolg sehr wichtig. Deshalb enthält die Rubrik *Was wissen Sie noch?* Aufgaben, die Sie zu den Hör- und Lesetexten des Kursbuches zurückführen. Bei den Hörtexten zum Arbeitsbuch finden Sie sowohl die entsprechenden Hörtexte aus dem Kursbuch als auch zusätzliche Hörtexte, mit denen Sie das Hörverstehen üben können.

Aussprache
Das Arbeitsbuch bietet Ihnen in jeder Lektion Aufgaben zur Aussprache. Dort können Sie systematisch die Satzintonation, den Satz- und Wortakzent sowie die Aussprache einzelner Laute trainieren.

Schreibwerkstatt
Auf der letzten Seite jeder Arbeitsbuchlektion finden Sie unter der Rubrik *Schreibwerkstatt* Aufgaben zum Schreiben. Die Schreibaufgaben sind so gestaltet, dass Sie dabei auch die Grammatik, den Wortschatz und die Redemittel der jeweiligen Lektion im Rahmen einer authentischen Schreibsituation üben können.

Piktogramme und Symbole

A1 Diese Verweise zeigen Ihnen, zu welchen Teilen im Kursbuch die Aufgaben im Arbeitsbuch passen.

▶ 103 Dieses Symbol verweist auf einen Hörtext. Sie finden alle Hörtexte zu den Aufgaben im Arbeitsbuch im MP3-Format im Lehrwerkservice unter www.hueber.de/motive.

Lisa spielt nicht gern Tennis ...
Schreiben Sie die Lösung zu dieser Aufgabe bitte auf ein Blatt Papier oder in ein Heft.

Die Tipps geben Ihnen nützliche Hinweise zum Selbstlernen.

→ Hier können Sie weiterlernen: www.hueber.de/motive
Im Internet finden Sie im Bereich *Lernen* weitere Übungen, die Lösungen zu den Aufgaben im Arbeitsbuch, die Transkriptionen zu allen Hörtexten und weiteres Material.

Inhalt

Lernwortschatz

Einstiegsseite
der/das Blog, -s
die Erfahrung, -en
der Kommentar, -e
der Kontakt, -e
das Netzwerk, -e
die Postkarte, -n

bloggen
simsen
twittern

selten
sozial

einen Blog schreiben
Freunde im sozialen Netzwerk treffen
in Kontakt bleiben
eine Postkarte schicken
pro
soziales Netzwerk, soziale Netzwerke
zurzeit

A1
die Jahreszahl, -en
das Smartphone, -s
das Fax(gerät), -e
das Radiohören

benutzen

möglich

dass
möglich sein
sicher sein

A2
der Anrufer, -
die Anruferin, -nen
der Ausflug, ⸚e
die Mailbox, -en
der Möbelwagen, -
die Wanderung, -en

zurückrufen

die Mailbox von …
für halb eins reserviert
Möbel bekommen
essen gehen
für eine Kollegin arbeiten

A3
hinterlassen

eine Nachricht hinterlassen
… gefällt … wohl besser
wohl

A4
der Rückruf, -e

jemanden zu einem Essen einladen
jemanden zu einer Party einladen
mit jemandem zu einem Konzert gehen
Hilfe brauchen
Nachrichten auf der Mailbox
von einem Freund erzählen

… will etwas von Ihnen wissen
… möchte einen Rückruf

B1
die Bildunterschrift, -en
das Cybermobbing
der Dritte, -n
der Filzstift, -e
die Generation, -en
der/die Jugendliche, -n
der Leiter, -
die Leiterin, -nen
der Leser, -
das Mobbing
das Netz, -e
die Note, -n
das Opfer, -
der Schulleiter, -
das Schulprojekt, -e
der Täter, -

anfangen
aufräumen
diskutieren
entschuldigen
löschen
passieren

böse
dumm
einfach
fleißig
gefährlich
hässlich

alles ist anders
auf keinen Fall
einfach im Bett bleiben
besonders einfach
etwas gegen etwas tun
fast
ganz
na ja
Nachrichten löschen
schlechte Späße machen
Probleme mit … haben
Schüler mit guten Noten
sondern
zur Schule gehen

B2
das Blatt, ⸚er

abgeben
gewinnen
unterschreiben
wiedersehen

nett
typisch

gerade

C1
der Bescheid
der Gasthof, ⸚e
die Hochzeit, -en
die Hochzeitsreise, -n
der Mitarbeiter, -
der Spielplatz, ⸚e

das Standesamt, ⸚er
der Verwandtenbesuch, -e

annehmen
Bescheid sagen/geben
feiern
heiraten
hoffen
stattfinden

C2
der Führerschein, -e
CH: der Führerausweis, -e
der Lehrer, -
die Prüfung, -en
der Umzug, ⸚e
die Vorbereitung, -en
der Wunsch, ⸚e

absagen
bestehen
umziehen
A: übersiedeln
CH: zügeln
wünschen
zusagen

herzlich
pünktlich

den Führerschein machen
eine Prüfung bestehen
bei den Vorbereitungen helfen
bei mir zu Hause

A

A1 **1 Ergänzen Sie und ordnen Sie die Bilder zu.**

1 2 3 4 5 6 7 8 9

a	7	einen _ r _ _ f schreiben	e		_ w _ t t _ _ _
b		eine N _ c h r _ c h t als SMS schicken, _ i m s _ _	f		einen B _ _ g schreiben, _ l o _ _ e n
			g		eine P o _ _ k _ _ _ _ schicken
c		t _ l _ f o _ _ _ _ _ _ _, jemanden a _ r u _ _ _	h		Freunde im s _ z _ _ l e n N _ t z w _ _ k treffen
d		c h _ _ _ _ _	i		am Computer s k _ _ _ _

2 Lesen Sie und ergänzen Sie die fehlenden Wörter.

Nur keinen Stress!

Im Sommer bin ich in meinem Ferienhaus. Ich habe dort keinen C o m p u t e r (a), kein F _ _ g e r ä t (b) und kein T _ _ _ _ _ _ (c). Auch mein H _ _ _ _ (d) nehme ich nicht mit. Das heißt, ich s k _ _ _ (e) nicht, ich t _ _ _ _ _ _ _ _ _ _ (f) nicht, ich c h _ _ _ _ (g) nicht, ich s i _ _ _ (h) nicht und ich bin in keinem s _ _ _ _ _ e n N _ _ _ _ _ _ _ (i). Ich schreibe nur P _ _ _ k _ _ _ _ _ (j) und B r _ _ _ _ (k). Meine Freunde finden das manchmal gar nicht gut. Sie möchten immer in Kontakt bleiben. Das ist aber nicht möglich, denn im Sommer mag ich keinen Stress. Meine Freunde können meine Nachbarin a _ _ _ _ _ _ (l) und dort eine N _ _ _ _ _ _ _ _ (m) für mich abgeben. Und sie können Briefe schreiben. Ich schreibe auch sicher einen Antwortbrief.

3 Sind die Sätze richtig oder falsch? Was meinen Sie? Kreuzen Sie an und schreiben Sie *dass*-Sätze wie im Beispiel. Vergleichen Sie dann mit der Lösung.

		richtig	falsch
a	Ein Brief aus dem Jahr 1847, der „Bordeaux-Brief“, kostet heute 20 Millionen Euro.		
b	Es gibt seit 1957 Anrufbeantworter.		
c	Alle Internetnutzer kaufen im Internet ein.		
d	Die Vorwahl für einen Anruf nach Deutschland ist 0049.		
e	Nur wenige Menschen finden Computer schön (25 %).		
f	Die meisten Internetnutzer leben in Asien.		

	dass-Satz dass		Verb
a Ich glaube nicht,	dass	der „Bordeaux-Brief“ heute 20 Millionen Euro	kostet.
b Ich glaube,	dass	...	

Lösung
a Falsch: Er kostet 10 Millionen Euro. Auf dem Brief sind zwei sehr teure Briefmarken.
b Richtig.
c Falsch: Nicht alle, aber sehr viele Internetnutzer kaufen auch im Internet ein (80%).
d Richtig.
e Falsch: 87 % finden Computer schön.
f Richtig: In Asien benutzen über 900 Millionen Menschen das Internet, in Europa nur 500 Millionen.

Tipp Grammatik
Nach *dass* kommt ein Nebensatz. In einem Nebensatz steht das Verb am Satzende. In den nächsten Lektionen lernen Sie noch andere Wörter mit Nebensatz kennen. Lernen Sie diese Wörter gut und markieren Sie:

dass + Nebensatz

4 Wer sagt was? Ordnen Sie zu und schreiben Sie *dass*-Sätze.

a ~~Herr Lehmann~~: — „Ich skype jeden Tag mit meinem Mann.“
b Julia und Sonja: — „Ich habe noch nie eine Postkarte geschrieben.“
c Torsten: — „Meine Mutter ruft mich jedes Wochenende an.“
d Frau Herbst: — „Wir möchten auf unserer Reise einen Blog schreiben.“
e Kerstin: — „Zwei Monate ohne Computer waren eine interessante Erfahrung für mich.“
f Ralf: — „~~Im Büro darf ich mein Smartphone nicht benutzen.~~“

a Herr Lehmann sagt, dass <u>er</u> im Büro <u>sein</u> Smartphone nicht benutzen darf. b ...

A2 **5** **Hören Sie die Nachrichten auf der Mailbox und vergleichen Sie sie mit den Notizen. In jeder Notiz gibt es einen Fehler. Korrigieren Sie die Fehler.**

103–106

a
Ausflug und
Wanderung am
Samstag
Zug: Abfahrt
~~9:30 Uhr~~ 9:55 Uhr

b
Einkaufsliste
Norbert: Salat,
Karotten, Milch
Irmgard: Brot, Wurst

c
Krankenhaus
Unfall mit dem
Fahrrad
fertig: halb zwei

d
Daniel + Karin,
Frankreich
Donnerstag zurück
Haustür offen?

6 **Welche Fehler haben die Personen in 5 gemacht? Schreiben Sie *dass*-Sätze.**

a (Zug – abfahren) Christine sagt, dass der Zug um 9:55 Uhr abfährt.
Markus schreibt, dass ...

b (... – kaufen) Norbert sagt, dass er ...
Irmgard schreibt, dass Norbert ...

c (fertig sein) Tim sagt, dass er ...
Seine Mutter schreibt, dass Tim ...

d (... – offen sein) Daniel sagt, dass ...
Monika schreibt, dass ...

> **Tipp Grammatik**
> Trennbare Verben bleiben im Nebensatz zusammen.
> Aussagesatz: *Der Zug fährt um 9:55 Uhr ab.*
> Nebensatz: *Christine sagt, dass der Zug um 9:55 Uhr abfährt.*

7 **In 5 sind vier Themen (a–c) wichtig. Ordnen Sie die Wörter den Themen zu und schreiben Sie bei den Nomen auch den Artikel und den Plural. Finden Sie noch weitere Wörter zu den Themen.**

Bus ~~Käse~~ U-Bahn Medikament Orangensaft ankommen
Kühlschrank Grad ~~Arzt~~ Kartoffel ~~Fahrrad~~ Ei schmecken Auto
Fleisch Praxis zu Fuß gehen Flugzeug Schmerzen Fieber Straßenbahn
~~Wind~~ Sonne heiß Apotheke Gepäck Gute Besserung!

a Verkehrsmittel: das Fahrrad (¨-er), ..., der Zug (¨-e), ...
b Lebensmittel: der Käse, ..., der Salat (-e), ...
c Gesundheit: der Arzt (¨-e), ..., das Krankenhaus (¨-er), ...
d Wetter: der Wind (-e), ..., regnen, ...

> **Tipp Wortschatz**
> Wiederholen Sie den Wortschatz aus den Lektionen 1–8. Sie brauchen die Wörter auch in den nächsten Lektionen.

A3 **8** **Eine Nachricht auf der Mailbox. Ergänzen Sie die Verben. Welche Antwort möchte Rolf hören? Kreuzen Sie an.**

~~sind~~ haben ... gegessen Könnt ... abholen sind ... gewandert haben ... gemacht gibt

Hallo Susanne,
hier ist Rolf. Wir sind (a) hier am Bahnhof in Feldbach. Wir ______ am Vormittag zum Schloss ______ (b). Am Nachmittag ______ wir eine Führung im Schloss ______ (c), und am Abend ______ wir im Schlossrestaurant gut ______ (d). Aber jetzt ______ (e) es keinen Zug nach Hause. ______ ihr uns mit dem Auto ______ (f)? Bitte ruf zurück.

1 ☐ Hallo Rolf, ihr könnt ja in Feldbach übernachten. Morgen gibt es sicher einen Zug.
2 ☐ Hallo Rolf, alles klar. Wir sind in einer halben Stunde bei euch.

9 **Welche Verben in 8 stehen im Perfekt? Wie heißt der Infinitiv? Schreiben Sie.**

Perfekt	Infinitiv
sind ... gewandert, ...	wandern, ...

B

B1 **1** Was wissen Sie noch? Lesen Sie noch einmal → KB S. 72, B1b. Was passt? Unterstreichen Sie die richtigen Wörter.

Kevin (ist) immer / selten (a) gern zur Schule (gegangen). Er hatte auch immer gute/schlechte (b) Noten. Doch dann ist er der Täter / das Opfer (c) von Cybermobbing geworden. Zuerst waren nette/dumme (d) SMS auf seinem Handy, und dann hat er sein Foto in der Klasse / im Internet (e) gesehen. Jemand hat mit einem Filzstift eine lange, hässliche Nase / Brille (f) gezeichnet. Die Täter waren alle anonym/gefährlich (g). Am ersten Tag ist Kevin den ganzen Tag im Bett / Schwimmbad (h) geblieben und hat nur an das Foto im Netz gedacht. Seine Eltern sind mit ihm zur Polizei/Schulleiterin (i) gegangen. Gemeinsam haben sie eine Lösung gefunden / die Handynachrichten gelöscht (j). In der Schule haben die Jugendlichen/Eltern (k) Projekte gemacht und über das Problem Cybermobbing gesprochen.

2 Markieren Sie in 1 die Perfekt-Formen und ordnen Sie sie dann zu. Schreiben Sie auch die Infinitive.

ge-...-en	ge-...-t
ist gegangen (gehen), ist geworden (werden), ...	hat ...

3 Ordnen Sie die Verben zu und schreiben Sie die Perfekt-Formen. Ergänzen Sie dann die Regeln.

~~schreiben~~ ~~zeigen~~ warten finden zählen fahren suchen geben fragen kaufen leben nehmen hören

ge-...-en	ge-...-t
schreiben – hat geschrieben, ...	zeigen – hat gezeigt, ...

Regeln

Einige wichtige Verben Einige wichtige Verben Die meisten Verben Die meisten Verben

a ______________ bilden das Partizip mit *ge-...-t*.
______________ bilden das Partizip mit *ge-...-en*. Diese Verben müssen Sie gut lernen.

b ______________ bilden das Perfekt mit *haben*.
______________ bilden das Perfekt mit *sein*. Diese Verben müssen Sie gut lernen.

B2 **4** Ergänzen Sie die E-Mails. Welche Nachrichten finden Sie nett ☺, welche finden Sie nicht so nett ☹? Ergänzen Sie die Smileys.

a ~~sind abgeflogen~~ hat ... abgeholt mitgekommen seid haben ... ausgepackt sind ... angekommen

Hallo Eveline, ◯

wir sind um 12:30 Uhr abgeflogen und ________ um 15:00 Uhr in Paris ________. Pierre ________ uns vom Flughafen ________. Wir sind zurzeit im Hotel. Wir ________ auch schon unsere Koffer ________. Wir denken an Euch! Es tut uns sehr leid, dass Ihr nicht ________ ________!

Liebe Grüße aus Paris
Luise und Axel

b haben ... zurückgerufen habe ... angerufen haben ... eingeladen haben ... zugehört

Hallo Herr Jung, ◯

ich ________ Sie schon viermal ________. Warum ________ Sie nicht ________? Sie ________ Dr. Witzigmann von der Firma Epstein nicht zu unserer Feier ________.
Sie ________ gestern in der Firma wohl nicht ________: Es ist wichtig, dass er kommt! Nicht nur für mich, sondern auch für alle Mitarbeiter. Ich will Sie morgen um halb acht in meinem Büro sehen.

H. Hubmann

5 Finden Sie in jedem Satz einen Fehler und korrigieren Sie ihn.

a Wann ~~hast~~ bist du gestern nach Hause gekommen?
b Wir haben gestern fleißig lernen.
c Anton und Tine ist am Wochenende gewandert.
d Herr Neumann hat eine E-Mail schreiben.
e Er hat eine Stunde lang wartet.
f Seid ihr gestern Tennis gespielt?

6 Schreiben Sie das Perfekt.

aufräumen hat aufgeräumt
fernsehen ______
anfangen ______
ausgehen ______
anziehen ______
aussehen ______

7 Ergänzen Sie die Verben aus 6 im Perfekt.

a • Warum hast du deinen Mantel nicht ______?
▪ Ich brauche ihn nicht. Es ist heute nicht kalt.

b • Warum siehst du so müde aus?
▪ Ich ______ gestern sehr lange ______. Der Krimi war wirklich gut.

c • Komm schnell, wir kommen zu spät.
▪ Auf keinen Fall, das Konzert ______ sicher noch nicht ______.

d • Peters Zimmer sieht sehr schön aus.
▪ Ja, er ______ es endlich ______.

e • Wo wart ihr am Samstagabend?
▪ Wir ______ ______, wir waren in der Disco.

f • Antonia hat Fieber und liegt im Bett.
▪ Ja, sie ______ gestern schon krank ______.

8 Ordnen Sie die Verben zu und schreiben Sie das Perfekt.

verlieren gefallen ~~beginnen~~ entfernen reparieren besuchen übernachten entschuldigen unterschreiben verkaufen erraten telefonieren verdienen gewinnen bekommen überweisen diskutieren erlauben passieren erzählen bezahlen gehören verstehen

be-: hat begonnen, ..
er-: ______
ent-: ______
ver-: ______
ge-: ______
über-: ______
unter-: ______
-ieren: ______

Tipp Grammatik
Verben mit den Vorsilben *be-*, *er-*, *ent-*, *ver-* und Verben auf *-ieren* haben im Perfekt kein *-ge-*.

9 Schreiben Sie Fragen wie im Beispiel und machen Sie ein Interview mit einer/einem Bekannten. Notieren Sie die Antworten.

a mit einem Politiker diskutieren
b ein Handy verlieren
c mit einem anderen Namen unterschreiben
d im Bus die Fahrkarte nicht bezahlen
e eine falsche Geschichte erzählen
f in einem Zelt übernachten
g bei einem Glücksspiel gewinnen

a Hast du schon einmal mit einem Politiker diskutiert? (Wann? Wo?) – Ja, im Herbst, vor unserem Rathaus.
b ...

C1 **1 Gertrude Keller hat zwei Einladungen bekommen. Ordnen Sie die Textteile (a–f) den Einladungen (1–2) zu.**

1

a, ...

2

~~a~~ 40 wird man nicht jedes Jahr! Deshalb muss man auch richtig feiern ... Das mache ich am 5. 6. im Gasthof Berger.

b Liebe Gerti, unser Haus ist endlich fertig. Nächste Woche ziehen wir um! Wir können also schon diesen Winter in den eigenen „vier Wänden" wohnen. Das möchten wir am 20. 9. gemeinsam mit Euch und anderen Freunden feiern.

c Wir beginnen um 15:00 Uhr und hoffen, dass das Wetter schön ist. Denn wir möchten Euch natürlich auch unseren Garten zeigen. Bei Regen feiern wir im Haus.

d Kein Problem, wir haben ja jetzt genug Platz! Wir hoffen, dass Ihr kommen könnt. Gebt uns bitte Bescheid. Herzliche Grüße, Anna

e Dort treffen wir uns um halb eins zum Mittagessen. Am Nachmittag sind schon zwei Tennisplätze gemietet und für die Wanderer gibt es eine Bergtour.

f Am Abend geht's dann richtig los, ... mit Livemusik! Wollt Ihr übernachten? Dann ruft mich an. Ich reserviere dort ein Zimmer für Euch. Peter

2 Gertrudes Mann hat viele Fragen. Welche Fragen passen zu Einladung 1 (Geburtstag), welche zu Einladung 2 (Umzug)? Ergänzen Sie und kreuzen Sie an.

~~Sollen~~ Wie Müssen Haben Wie lange Was Wie viel Wo

			Einladung 1	Einladung 2
a	Sollen	wir Anna etwas für den Garten schenken?	☐	X
b	______	kommt man zum Gasthof Berger?	☐	☐
c	______	sie auch ein Schwimmbad im Garten?	☐	☐
d	______	wünscht sich Peter zum Geburtstag?	☐	☐
e	______	wohnt Anna jetzt?	☐	☐
f	______	dauert das Fest bei Anna?	☐	☐
g	______	wir am Abend tanzen?	☐	☐
h	______	kostet ein Zimmer im Gasthof Berger?	☐	☐

3 Was will Gertrudes Mann wissen? Schreiben Sie die Fragen aus 2 noch einmal wie im Beispiel.

	indirekter Fragesatz „ob" oder Fragewort		Verb
a Gertrudes Mann will wissen,	ob	sie Anna etwas für den Garten	schenken sollen.
b Er will wissen,	wie	...	

Tipp Grammatik
Auch indirekte Fragesätze sind Nebensätze.
Das Verb steht immer an letzter Position.

4 Was sagen die Personen? Schreiben Sie die Sätze in die Sprechblasen.

a

Henrik fragt Annette, wie spät es ist.
Annette fragt Henrik, ob er keine Uhr hat.

b

Der Kellner fragt die Frau, ob sie etwas essen möchte.
Die Frau fragt, ob es Suppe gibt.

c

Die Frau fragt den Verkäufer, wie viel das Kleid kostet.
Der Verkäufer fragt die Frau, welches Kleid sie meint.

d

Der Mann möchte wissen, wie er zum Hauptplatz kommt. Der andere Mann fragt, ob er mit dem Bus fahren oder zu Fuß gehen will.

5 Partyvorbereitungen. Ergänzen Sie die Verben im Präsens oder im Perfekt.
In welchen Dialogen sprechen die Gäste (G)? Markieren Sie.

a [G] • Hast du ihre Adresse *aufgeschrieben*?
▪ Du hast gesagt, dass du sie aufschreibst.

b [–] • Hast du schon für die Party eingekauft?
▪ Nein, ich ______ morgen ______.

c [ ] • Sind wir pünktlich oder ______ die Party schon ______?
▪ Nein, sie fängt erst in einer Stunde an.

d [ ] • Hast du das Geschenk schon eingepackt?
▪ Nein, das ______ ich im Auto ______.

e [ ] • ______ du deine Mutter schon ______?
▪ Nein, die lade ich heute Abend noch ein.

f [ ] • Warum ______ du eine kurze Hose ______?
▪ Wir fahren zu einer Grillparty. Warum soll ich keine kurze Hose anziehen?

g [ ] • Hast du die Getränke vom Großmarkt abgeholt?
▪ Nein, die ______ ich am Nachmittag ______.

h [ ] • ______ du die 20 Grillhähnchen ______?
▪ Ich rufe im Supermarkt an und hole sie gleich ab.

Aussprache

▶ 107 Hören Sie und markieren Sie die Satzmelodie (→ ↘ ↗).

a Weißt du, [→] wann die Hochzeit beginnt? [↗]
Beginnt sie um neun [ ] oder erst um zehn? [ ]
Ich frage mich, [ ] ob Jasmin auch zum Standesamt kommt. [ ]
Was meinst du? [ ] Hat Karin sie auch eingeladen? [ ]

b Weißt du, [ ] wie man zum Standesamt kommt? [ ]
Ich hoffe, [ ] dass wir nicht weit fahren müssen. [ ]

c Sag mir bitte, [ ] was ich anziehen soll. [ ]
Soll ich den Rock [ ] oder soll ich doch lieber das Kleid anziehen? [ ]

Schreibwerkstatt

1 Livia hat eine Einladung von ihrer Freundin Anita bekommen. Lesen Sie Livias Antwort und beantworten Sie die Fragen.

a Was für eine Einladung hat Livia bekommen? ______

b Kann Livia zusagen oder muss sie absagen? Warum? ______

Liebe Anita,

vielen Dank für Deine E-Mail. Wir haben uns wirklich schon lange nicht gesehen. Es ist schön, dass es Euch so gut geht. Bei uns ist auch alles o. k. Ich habe ganz vergessen, dass Deine Kinder schon so groß sind. Emma ist 15, und Kevin sogar schon 18. Ich kann es nicht glauben! Du sagst, dass Kevin die Führerscheinprüfung bestanden hat. Ich sehe ihn noch mit seinem Kinderfahrrad vor mir.
Du arbeitest jetzt also wieder als Krankenschwester. Ich kann das gut verstehen. Du hast Dir das ja schon so lange gewünscht. Du sagst, dass Du auch in der Nacht arbeiten musst. Das ist sicher nicht einfach. Und dann hast Du auch noch ein Straßenfest organisiert. Ich glaube Dir gern, dass das viel Arbeit war. Und das alles neben Deinem Beruf!
Übrigens vielen Dank für die Einladung zu Eurem Straßenfest. Leider können wir nicht kommen. Am Samstag sind wir in Köln bei meiner Mutter. Sie feiert ihren sechzigsten Geburtstag. Euer Fest beginnt um 14:00 Uhr, da sitzen wir schon im Auto. Es tut mir wirklich leid, dass wir uns nicht wiedersehen. Aber vielleicht habt Ihr nächste Woche Zeit. Besucht uns doch am Wochenende.

Liebe Grüße und viel Spaß bei Eurem Fest
Livia

2 Lesen Sie noch einmal. Was meinen Sie? Was hat Anita in ihrer Einladung geschrieben? Machen Sie Notizen zu den Themen.

a Livia und Anita: lange nicht gesehen; ...

b Anitas Kinder: Tochter Emma ...

c Anitas Beruf: ______

d Anitas Arbeit für das Straßenfest: ______

e das Straßenfest (Wochentag und Uhrzeit): ______

3 Schreiben Sie jetzt die Einladung von Anita an Livia.

Liebe Livia,
wir haben uns lange nicht gesehen. Uns geht es gut. Wie ...

4 Anita möchte Livia wiedersehen. Sie schreibt noch eine E-Mail. Lesen Sie, was Anita wissen möchte.

Anita möchte wissen, ...
– wie die Geburtstagsfeier war.
– ob Livia am nächsten Wochenende Zeit hat.
– wann sie Livia besuchen kann.
– wo Livia wohnt.
– ob Livia vielleicht lieber zu ihr kommen möchte.
Anita bittet Livia, dass sie bald schreibt.

5 Schreiben Sie Anitas E-Mail.

Liebe Livia,
wie war die Geburtstagsfeier bei Deiner Mutter? Ihr hattet sicher viel Spaß.
...

→ Hier können Sie weiterlernen: www.hueber.de/motive

Lernwortschatz

Einstiegsseite
der Kindergarten, ¨
das Rad, ¨er

blond
dunkel
jung

gut essen

A1
das Argument, -e
das Aussehen
die Figur
die Haarfarbe, -n
die Industrie
die Kosmetik
die Kosmetik-industrie
die Kranken-versicherung, -en
die Medizin
die Modefirma, -firmen
die Operation, -en
die Schönheit
die Schönheits-operation, -en
der Unfall, ¨e
die Verletzung, -en
die Versicherung, -en

akzeptieren
ändern
enden
kämpfen
korrigieren
retten
sterben
versprechen
zählen

eng
dick
dünn
jugendlich
schlank
schwer
ungefährlich
unglücklich
unzufrieden

absolut
dafür sein
dagegen sein
damit
eher
einig-
für etwas sein
gegen etwas sein
mindestens
selbst
so ... wie
die schwere Verletzung
zum Glück

A2
der Anzug, ¨e
die Bluse, -n
der Handschuh, -e
die Handtasche, -n
die Kappe, -n
das Kleidungs-stück, -e
der Rock, ¨e
CH: der Jupe, -s
die Saison
die Socke, -n
A/CH: der Socken, -
der Stiefel, -
die Zeile, -n

behalten

dunkel
hell
praktisch

B1
die Angst, ¨e
die Spülmaschine, -n
A/CH: der Geschirrspüler, -

ausräumen
geben
zumachen

eilig
leise

Angst haben
die Spülmaschine ausräumen
mit Milch und Zucker

B2
die Größe, -n

versuchen
probieren

B3
egal
froh

C1
der Eindruck
die Stimme, -n

aktiv
energisch
faul
hübsch
intelligent
komisch
optimistisch
pessimistisch
sportlich
sympathisch
unwichtig
unsympathisch

als

C2
das Verkehrsmittel, -
die Zeitschrift, -en

C3
der Autofahrer, -
der Chatroom, -s
die Luft
die Meinung, -en
der Radfahrer, -
CH: der Velofahrer, -
das Rauchverbot
der Tipp, -s
die Umwelt
der Verkehr

attraktiv
gemütlich
rauchfrei
sicher

am besten
gleich

A1 **1** **Was wissen Sie noch? Lesen Sie noch einmal** → KB S. 78, A1b **und ordnen Sie zu. Achtung: Drei Satzhälften passen nicht.**

a Schönheitsinstitute versprechen,
b Sehr viele Deutsche kaufen
c Das argentinische Starmodel Solange Magnano
d Nach einem Unfall mit schweren Verletzungen
e Die Krankenversicherung bezahlt

1 kann oft nur eine Schönheitsoperation helfen.
2 dass sie ihre Kunden schöner und jünger machen.
3 ist absolut gegen die Kosmetikindustrie.
4 dass sie keine Mode- und Kosmetikprodukte verkaufen.
5 nach einem Unfall auch die Schönheitsoperation.
6 ist nach einer Schönheitsoperation gestorben.
7 sind Schönheitsoperationen ungefährlich.
8 jedes Jahr für viel Geld ihr Wunschaussehen.

A2 **2** **Lesen Sie und ordnen Sie die Namen den Zeichnungen zu.**

S = Steffi T = Tina D = David

a Steffis Nase ist länger als Tinas Nase.
b Davids Nase ist kürzer als Tinas Nase.
c Davids Augen sind kleiner als Steffis Augen.
d Tinas Augen sind größer als Steffis Augen.
e Davids Mund ist kleiner als Steffis Mund.
f Steffis Mund ist so groß wie Tinas Mund, Tina hat aber einen Schönheitsfleck (= Punkt).

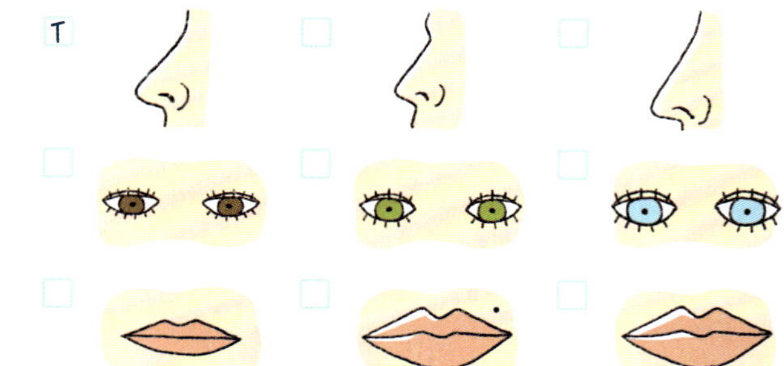

3 **Unterstreichen Sie die Komparative in 2. Schreiben Sie dann die Sätze a–e noch einmal wie im Beispiel. Benutzen Sie die Gegenteile der Adjektive *(klein ↔ groß)*.**

a Tinas Nase ist kürzer als Steffis Nase. b ...

4 **Ergänzen Sie den Komparativ.**

	Komparativ		Komparativ
langweilig	langweiliger	gesund	gesünder
laut		viel	
alt		gern	
kalt		gut	

Tipp Grammatik
Die Regel für den Komparativ ist einfach: Adjektiv + *-er (klein – kleiner)*.
Aber die Regel stimmt nicht immer.
Lernen Sie: *viel – mehr, gern – lieber, gut – besser*
Einige (kurze) Adjektive:
a, o, u → ä, ö, ü (groß – größer)

5 **Ergänzen Sie die Komparative aus 4.**

a Das Buch finde ich toll, den Film finde ich eher nicht so gut. Er ist langweiliger als das Buch.
b Dieses Jahr ist der Winter ________ als letztes Jahr. Man kann Skifahren, das war letztes Jahr nicht möglich.
c Ich gehe lieber zum Fußballspiel als ins Konzert, das macht ________ Spaß.
d Wir wohnen jetzt direkt neben dem Bahnhof. In unserer neuen Wohnung ist es ________ als in der alten Wohnung.
e Andreas spielt ________ Tennis als ich. Meistens verliere ich gegen ihn.
f Mein Bruder ist ________ als ich. Ich bin 26, er ist 30.
g Ich nehme den Fisch, der ist ________ als der Hamburger.
h Mein Mann mag Fußball, aber ich sehe ________ Krimis als Sportsendungen.

6 **... *als* oder *so ... wie*? Schreiben Sie Sätze.**

a klein: Alexanders Wohnung – 80 m² / Susannes Wohnung – 120 m²
b lang: Winterurlaub – 14 Tage / Sommerurlaub – 2 Wochen
c schnell: Zugfahrt – 3 Stunden 30 Minuten / Flug – 1 Stunde 15 Minuten (Berlin – Frankfurt)
d alt: Herr Meier – 32 Jahre / Frau Schober – 32 Jahre
e billig: „Moli"-Orangensaft (2 Liter) – 2 € / „Bali"-Orangensaft (½ Liter) – 45 Cent

a Alexanders Wohnung ist ... als ...

7 **Lesen Sie und vergleichen Sie die Fitnesscenter. Schreiben Sie Sätze wie im Beispiel.**

~~zentral (= im Zentrum)~~ Trainer (viel) lange geöffnet groß alt
Trainingsgeräte (modern) billig gut gefallen

A

Fit mach mit
Fitnesscenter im Stadtzentrum

- persönliches Training mit Gabi oder Toni
- 250 m²
- Dienstag und Donnerstag: Aerobic

Öffnungszeiten: 9:00–22:00 Uhr
30,– Euro monatlich

B

Kraft und Co. – Ihr Fitnesscenter
Neueröffnung im EZ Süd,
nur 10 km vom Stadtzentrum

- 10 Trainer
- 800 m²
- ultramoderne Trainingsgeräte
- sechs Kurse täglich

Öffnungszeiten: 6:00–24:00 Uhr
45,– Euro pro Monat

Das Fitnesscenter „Fit mach mit" (A) liegt zentraler als das Fitnesscenter „Kraft und Co." (B).
Das Fitnesscenter B hat ... Trainer als ...

8 **Ordnen Sie die Gegenteile zu.**

~~groß~~ interessant alt schlank kurz ruhig schlecht gefährlich hässlich
bekannt warm gut zufrieden jung unzufrieden laut weiß ungefährlich
~~klein~~ schön lang unbekannt kalt dick bunt langweilig

groß – klein, ...

9 **Vergleichen Sie. Schreiben Sie persönliche Sätze mit den Adjektiven aus 8 wie im Beispiel.**

a meine Heimatstadt – eine andere Stadt (z. B. New York)
b der Winter in meinem Heimatland – der Winter in Deutschland
c meine Lieblingsmusik – andere Musik
d mein Lieblingsrestaurant – andere Restaurants
e Urlaubszeit – Arbeitszeit
f ich – meine Freundin / mein Freund

a Meine Heimatstadt ist kleiner als New York. b ...

10 **Schreiben Sie die Nomen mit Artikel und Plural und ordnen Sie sie den Kleidungsstücken zu. Schreiben Sie auch die drei Adjektive.**

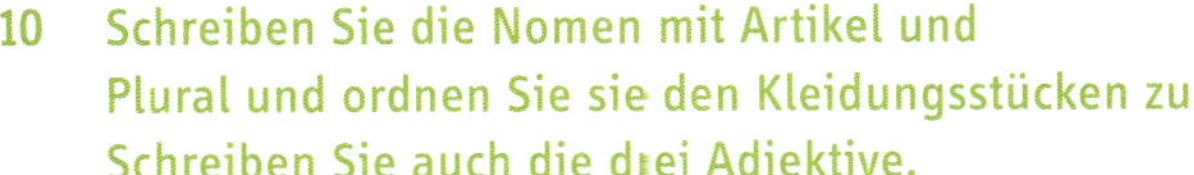

ppaKe akischprt oRck ~~ckSoe~~ nuAzg ndukel
schandheHu ieelStf lseuB llhe ndschtaHae

a die Socke (-n)
b ...
Adjektive: ...

11 **Vergleichen Sie. Welche Kleidungsstücke aus dem Kursbuch (Seite 79) fehlen in 10? Schreiben Sie die Wörter mit Artikel und Plural.**

Es fehlen: der Hut (¨-e), ...

B

B1 **1** **Was wissen Sie noch? Hören Sie noch einmal und kreuzen Sie an.**

▶ 108

a Der Verkäufer bringt Frau Roth
- ☐ Kaffee.
- ☐ Kleidungsstücke.
- ☐ einen Kunden.

b Frau Roth soll
- ☐ zwei Blusen enger machen.
- ☐ eine Hose kürzer machen.
- ☐ neue Pullover bestellen.

c Der Verkäufer meint,
- ☐ dass es zu viele Pullover in Größe XXXL gibt.
- ☐ dass die Pullover nicht in Ordnung sind.
- ☐ dass die Pullover zu klein sind.

d Die Kleider sollen
- ☐ am nächsten Tag
- ☐ nächste Woche
- ☐ in einer halben Stunde

fertig sein.

e Der Verkäufer
- ☐ hat einen Fehler gemacht.
- ☐ bekommt die Kleidungsstücke nicht pünktlich.
- ☐ braucht die Kleidungsstücke nicht mehr.

B2 **2** **Was passt? Ordnen Sie zu und schreiben Sie höfliche Fragen in der *ich*-Form wie im Beispiel.**

mit euch im Auto mitfahren   noch ein Mineralwasser haben
~~eine Nummer kleiner haben~~   ein Einzelzimmer haben   mit Ihnen den Platz tauschen
ein Medikament gegen Kopfschmerzen bekommen   die Rechnung haben

a ~~Die Schuhe sind zu groß.~~
b Sie möchten bezahlen.
c Sie möchten im Hotel übernachten.
d Sie möchten nicht zu Fuß gehen.
e Sie sind noch durstig.
f Sie möchten im Flugzeug nicht am Fenster sitzen.
g Sie haben Kopfschmerzen.

a Könnte ich die Schuhe eine Nummer kleiner haben? b …

3 **Ordnen Sie die Sätze den Bildern zu.**

1

2

3

a ~~Erklär mir das!~~
b Erzählt doch mal!
c Kommen Sie mit!
d Steigen Sie ein!
e Vergiss deine Tasche nicht!
f Helft mir bitte!

Bild	1	2	3
Satz	*a, …*		

▶ 109–114 **4** **Wer möchte was? Hören Sie und ordnen Sie die Wörter (1–6) den Situationen (a–f) zu. Schreiben Sie dann Imperative wie im Beispiel.**

1 mir die Fotos zeigen   2 zuhören   3 einsteigen   4 das für mich bezahlen
5 ~~noch Getränke mitbringen~~   6 am Nachmittag das Paket abholen

a 5 vor dem Fußballspiel: *Bring noch Getränke mit!*
b ☐ im Café: ____________
c ☐ an der Bushaltestelle: ____________
d ☐ zu Hause: ____________
e ☐ nach der Hochzeit: ____________
f ☐ auf der Reise: ____________

5 **Schreiben Sie die Imperative aus 4 höflicher.**

a Könntest du bitte Getränke mitbringen?
b Würdet ihr bitte …?

6 Im Restaurant oder im Kleidergeschäft? Was passt? Markieren Sie und kreuzen Sie an.

	im Restaurant	im Kleidergeschäft
a Ich nehme die Kappe / den Kuchen. Der sieht wirklich gut aus.	X	
b Die Schuhe / Die Pizza gefallen mir, die nehme ich.		
c Der Fisch / Die Hose schmeckt mir nicht. Den nehme ich sicher nicht.		
d Das Hemd / Der Salat sieht gut aus. Den nehme ich.		
e Das Kleid / Der Orangensaft passt mir nicht. Das nehme ich nicht.		

7 Wählen Sie ein Verb und schreiben Sie die Sätze aus 6 auch für die andere Situation (Restaurant ↔ Kleidergeschäft). Es gibt mehrere Möglichkeiten.

schmecken gefallen aussehen passen nehmen sein

a Ich nehme die Kappe. Die passt mir. b ...

8 Was sagt die Verkäuferin / der Verkäufer (V), was sagt die Kundin / der Kunde (K)? Ordnen Sie zu.

a K Ja, könnte ich ... probieren?
b V Guten Tag, kann ich Ihnen helfen?
c ☐ (Ich habe) Größe ...
d ☐ Der/Das/Die ... ist ein bisschen zu lang.
e ☐ Der/Das/Die ... passt mir nicht.
f ☐ Welche Größe brauchen Sie?
g ☐ Passt/Passen Ihnen der/das/die ...?
h ☐ Versuchen Sie mal Größe ...
i ☐ Könnte ich den/das/die ... eine Nummer größer/kleiner/weiter ... haben?
j ☐ Wie viel kostet der/das/die ...?
k ☐ Einen Moment. Ich bringe Ihnen den/das/die ... sofort.
l ☐ Wir können den/das/die ... kürzer machen.
m ☐ Ja, den/das/die ... nehme ich.
n ☐ Möchten Sie bar oder mit Kreditkarte bezahlen?

9 Wählen Sie mindestens zwei Situationen (a–d) und schreiben Sie Dialoge. Benutzen Sie die Sätze aus 8.

a Sie möchten eine Hose kaufen. Sie haben Größe 56. Sie probieren die Hose, aber sie ist zu lang.
b Sie möchten Schuhe kaufen. Sie haben Größe 41. Sie probieren die Schuhe, aber sie sind zu eng.
c Sie möchten einen Pullover kaufen. Sie haben Größe L. Sie probieren den Pullover, aber er ist zu weit.
d Sie möchten ein T-Shirt kaufen. Sie haben Größe S. Sie probieren das T-Shirt, aber es ist zu klein.

a ○ Guten Tag, kann ich Ihnen helfen?
△ Ja, könnte ich eine Hose probieren?
○ Welche ...

10 Einkaufen. Wie heißen die Fragen? Ergänzen Sie.

a ● Wie o___ k___ d___ Kl___?
■ Ich kaufe sehr selten Kleidung, vielleicht viermal im Jahr.
b ● K___ d___ g___ Kl___?
■ Nein, ich finde Kleidung kaufen langweilig, aber ich kaufe gern Bücher.
c ● M___ w___ g___ d___ g___ ei___?
■ Ich gehe gern mit meiner Freundin einkaufen. Sie weiß, was mir passt.
d ● S___ S___ f___ d___ w___?
■ Sonderangebote sind für mich nicht wichtig, die sind mir egal.
e ● B___ d___ Kl___ o___?
■ Ich bestelle nur Bücher und CDs online, Kleidung bestelle ich nie im Internet.
f ● W___ Kl___ k___ d___ g___?
■ Ich kaufe gern Schuhe. Da weiß ich meine Größe, und das dauert dann nicht so lange.

11 Schreiben Sie persönliche Antworten zu den Fragen aus 10.

C

C1 **1 Wie findest du sie? Wie ist er denn? Ordnen Sie die richtigen Gegenteile zu.**

a komisch/lustig	2	1	pessimistisch
b schön/hübsch/attraktiv		2	~~traurig/deprimiert~~
c ruhig		3	hässlich
d sympathisch		4	faul
e interessant		5	vorsichtig
f intelligent		6	nervös
g optimistisch		7	langweilig
h aktiv/energisch/fleißig		8	unsympathisch
i unvorsichtig		9	dumm

2 Ergänzen Sie die passenden Adjektive aus 1.

a Lorenz ist sehr p e s s i m _ _ _ _ _ _ _, er sieht überall Probleme.
b Stress ist für Anna kein Problem. Sie wird nie nervös und bleibt immer r _ _ _ _.
c Mit Albert haben wir immer viel Spaß, er ist sehr k _ _ _ _ _ _.
d Wir mögen unsere neuen Nachbarn nicht besonders, wir finden sie u _ _ _ _ _ _ _ _ _ _ _.
e Karin macht sehr viel Sport, sie ist sehr a _ _ _ _.
f Herr König lebt nicht gern gefährlich, er ist sehr v _ _ _ _ _ _ _ _ _.

C2 **3 Jana, Isabel und Juliane sind Schwestern. Wer ist wer (X, Y und Z)? Lesen Sie die Informationen über X, Y und Z. Ordnen Sie die Buchstaben den Namen zu und ergänzen Sie die fehlenden Informationen in der Tabelle.**

X ist am ältesten, sie ist 40 Jahre alt. Y ist acht Jahre jünger als X.
Z ist am größten. Sie ist 1 Meter 78 groß. Mit ihren 1 Meter 72 ist Y kleiner als X.
Y schwimmt am besten, Z spielt besser Golf als ihre Schwestern.

	Alter	Größe	Hobbys
Jana = ___	30 Jahre		Radfahren, Golf
Isabel = ___			Lesen, Schwimmen
Juliane = ___		1 Meter 76	Garten, Hockey, Geige

4 Schreiben Sie die Superlative.

~~alt~~ attraktiv gut groß gern schnell billig schwierig — am ältesten, am ...

5 Ergänzen Sie passende Superlative aus 4.

a Hugh Grant ist mein Lieblingsschauspieler. Ich finde, er sieht am attraktivsten aus.
b Ich nehme die Lasagne, die schmeckt hier ________.
c Diese Kamera war ________. Alle anderen Kameras waren teurer.
d In unserer Basketballmannschaft ist Mark ________. Er ist 2 Meter 10 groß.
e Mein Bruder ist 18 und meine Schwester 20 Jahre alt. Ich bin 23, ich bin ________.
f Ich koche gern. ________ koche ich am Wochenende, da habe ich genug Zeit dafür.

6 Vergleichen Sie. Wählen Sie je drei Nomen und ein Adjektiv und schreiben Sie Sätze wie im Beispiel.

a
Stiefel, Mantel, Jacke, Jeans, Rock, T-Shirt, Kleid, Pullover, Schuhe, Anzug

warm praktisch billig elegant

b
Bus, U-Bahn, Auto, Flugzeug, Zug, Schiff, Fahrrad

schnell langsam billig interessant praktisch

c

Salat

Fisch Zucker

Schokolade Kuchen

Tomaten Pommes frites

gesund teuer billig gut

d

Handy

Fernseher Radiergummi

Bleistift Wasserflasche

Computer Schreibtisch

groß praktisch hübsch interessant hässlich wichtig

a Die Jacke ist wärmer als der Pullover. Am wärmsten ist der Mantel. ...

C3 **7** Was wissen Sie noch? Lesen Sie noch einmal → KB S. 83, C3a. Ergänzen Sie die Komparative und ordnen Sie zu. Achtung: Drei Argumente passen nicht.

Meinungen		Argumente
a puma: Das Rauchverbot in Kneipen nervt.	2	1 Ich kämpfe gegen Rauchverbote. Ich will (frei) ______ leben.
b lady p.: Ich finde Rauchverbote in Restaurants gut. Ich bin dafür.		2 Früher war es in meiner Kneipe viel (gemütlich) gemütlicher.
c tabor: Ich mag keine Radfahrer in der Stadt.		3 Die Geschäfte gehen (schlecht) ______.
d ariadne: Noch mehr Autos in der Stadt? Ich bin dagegen.		4 Nichtraucher sind (attraktiv) ______. Das müssen auch die Raucher akzeptieren.
e stefan: Ich habe Angst. Ich verliere vielleicht meinen Job.		5 Als Autofahrer ist man (langsam) ______ als früher.
f fröhlich: Das ist doch egal. Such einen neuen Job.		6 Der ist vielleicht (interessant) ______ und du verdienst (viel) ______ Geld.
		7 Das Essen schmeckt dann dort (gut) ______.
		8 Die Stadt wird (sicher) ______ und die Luft wird (gut) ______.
		9 Wir retten die Umwelt und machen alle (glücklich) ______.

Aussprache

▶ 115 **1** Hören Sie. Wie oft können Sie im Text den *ich*-Laut finden? Unterstreichen Sie.

- Schau, die Hose ist wirklich günstig. Die möchte ich probieren.
- Aber wir haben es eilig. Um sechs haben wir den Termin bei Dr. Liebig, und wir sollten pünktlich sein.
- Sei nicht so stressig, das ist wirklich ungemütlich.
- Aber der Termin ist wichtig.
- Und die Hose ist sehr billig.
- Hoffentlich ist Dr. Liebig noch in seinem Büro.
- Natürlich, der ist doch so fleißig. Der arbeitet sicher noch.
- Gehen wir, der Termin ist wirklich wichtig. Und es ist möglich, dass …
- … Dr. Liebig nicht in seinem Büro ist. Bleib ganz ruhig, Felix und schau nach rechts.
- Dr. Liebig kauft hier ein!
- Das finde ich lustig.

▶ 116 **2** Wie schreibt man das? Hören Sie und sprechen Sie nach. Ergänzen Sie dann *-ig* oder *-ich*.

gefährl*ich* sportl___ langweil___ gemütl___ selbstständ___ wicht___
ruh___ glückl___ fleiß___ freundl___ hässl___ traur___

Schreibwerkstatt

▶ 117 **1** Tanja Gerber, eine gute Bekannte, möchte im Internet Kleider kaufen. Sie spricht auf Ihre Mailbox. Hören Sie und kreuzen Sie die richtigen Lösungen an.

a Tanja möchte im Internet ☐ eine Hose ☐ eine Bluse ☐ ein Kleid ☐ einen Mantel kaufen.
b Tanja möchte wissen, ☐ wie schnell man die Kleider bekommt. ☐ wie man am besten bezahlt. ☐ ob man die Kleider behalten muss.

2 Beantworten Sie Tanjas Fragen. Wählen Sie Argumente aus und schreiben Sie eine E-Mail.

⊕ Argumente für einen Kleiderkauf im Internet	⊖ Argumente gegen einen Kleiderkauf im Internet
Die Produkte sind manchmal billiger. Man kann auch am Sonntag oder in der Nacht einkaufen. Das ist praktischer. Man bekommt die Produkte mit der Post. …	Man kann die Kleidungsstücke nicht probieren. Verkäuferinnen und Verkäufer können nicht helfen. Der Umtausch ist schwieriger. Man muss zur Post gehen. …

Liebe Tanja,
ich kaufe gern / nicht gern im Internet ein.
Ein Einkauf im Internet ist praktischer/gefährlicher/schwieriger/einfacher/… als ein Einkauf im Geschäft. …
Man muss/kann …
Kauf ruhig im Internet ein. / Kauf lieber im Einkaufszentrum ein.
Viele/Liebe Grüße …

3 Am 23. Oktober: Die Firma Kleidermann schreibt an Tanja. Lesen Sie die E-Mail und beantworten Sie die Fragen.

Absender: Firma Kleidermann Empfänger: Tanja Gerber 23. Oktober
Betreff: AW: Umtausch

Sehr geehrte Frau Gerber,

Sie haben bei uns eine Hose und eine Bluse gekauft und möchten diese Kleidungsstücke umtauschen. Die Hose möchten Sie eine Nummer größer und die Bluse in einer anderen Farbe haben. Gern nehmen wir die Hose zurück. Die Bluse können wir aber leider nicht zurücknehmen. Ein Umtausch ist nur in den ersten 14 Tagen nach dem Kauf möglich. Sie haben die Hose vor zehn Tagen gekauft, die Bluse aber schon vor zwei Monaten. Wir hoffen, Sie verstehen die Situation.

Mit freundlichen Grüßen
Herta Bauer
Firma Kleidermann

a Was hat Tanja bei der Firma Kleidermann gekauft? ______
b Warum möchte sie die Kleidungsstücke umtauschen? ______
c Akzeptiert die Firma Kleidermann den Umtausch? Warum (nicht)? ______

4 Am 22. Oktober: Tanja hat an die Firma Kleidermann geschrieben. Was hat sie geschrieben? Schreiben Sie Tanjas E-Mail.

Absender: Tanja Gerber Empfänger: Firma Kleidermann 22. Oktober
Betreff: Umtausch

Sehr geehrte Damen und Herren,
ich habe … gekauft. … passt leider nicht / … ist zu klein.
Ich brauche … größer. Ich möchte … in Rot/Blau/…
Könnten Sie …? Ich schicke … zurück.
Mit freundlichen Grüßen

→ Hier können Sie weiterlernen: www.hueber.de/motive

Lernwortschatz

Einstiegsseite
das Einkaufszentrum, -zentren
die Städtereise, -n
der Stadtmensch, -en

spazieren gehen

A1
der Affe, -n
die Chefin, -nen
der Delfin, -e
der Elefant, -en
das Instrument, -e
der Pinguin, -e
die Robbe, -n
die Ruhe
die Sendung, -en
die Serie, -n
die Soap, -s
der Tiger, -
das Wildschwein, -e
die Wohngemeinschaft, -en
das Zebra, -s
der Zoo, -s
die Zoosendung, -en
das Zootier, -e
der Zuschauer, -

ausziehen
einziehen
handeln
zusammenleben

beliebt
höflich
unbeliebt
unhöflich

die Chefin spielen
manch-
seine Ruhe haben
zurück

A2
der Akku, -s
der Astronaut, -en
der Besucher, -
der Eisbär, -en
der Popstar, -s
die Sensation, -en
der Tierpfleger, -
der Zirkusdirektor, -en
der Zoobesucher, -
der Zookritiker, -

ansehen
A: anschauen
fotografieren
füttern
melden

A3
der Bär, -en
die Geburt, -en
der Star, -s

A4
der Ballon, -s/-e
der Direktor, -en
die Lüge, -n
das Motorrad, ¨-er
der Zirkus, -se

stimmen

B1
die Allergie, -n

aufpassen
freinehmen
riechen
stören

süß

weil

B2
die Batterie, -n
die Birne, -n
der CD-Player, -
der Drucker, -
die EC-Karte, -n
A: die Bankomatkarte, -n
die Heizung, -en
das Kabel, -
der Kopierer, -
das Licht, -er
der PIN-Code, -s
die Speicherkarte, -n
die Steckdose, -n
der Strom
die Taschenlampe, -n

funktionieren

voll

C1
das Formular, -e
die Grenze, -n
das Schaf, -e
der Schweizer, -

ausfüllen

meist-

C2
die Ahnung
das Blatt, ¨-er
das Dorf, ¨-er
das Feld, -er
das Huhn, ¨-er
die Katze, -n
die Kuh, ¨-e
die Landschaft, -en
die Mitte
der Mond
das Pferd, -e
die Pflanze, -n
der Schnee
das Schwein, -e
der Stern, -e
die Stimmung, -en
der Strand, ¨-e
das Tal, ¨-er
der Tierschützer, -
die USA (Pl.)
der Vogel, ¨
der Wald, ¨-er
der Wolf, ¨-e
die Wolke, -n

hinten
vorn(e)

A

A1 **1** Was wissen Sie noch? Lesen Sie noch einmal → KB S. 86, A1b. Ergänzen Sie die Namen (~~~) und die anderen Wörter (____).

Alma (eine Robbe)   Olli (ein Wildschwein)   Rada (ein Elefant)   Frau Peters

draußen   Jugendliche   unhöflich   Chefin   Ruhe   Sendung   akzeptieren   handeln   ~~Zoo~~   Wohngemeinschaft

a Letzte Woche (sollte) Frau Peters ihre Schwester (besuchen). Doch sie wollte lieber ihre Lieblingssendung „Pinguin, Robbe & Co." aus dem Düsseldorfer Zoo sehen. Die ________ zeigt, dass Tiere oft so fühlen und ________ wie wir, und das gefällt ~~~~~~~~.
b Früher durfte ~~~~~~~~ allein leben und hatte ihre ________. Doch vor drei Wochen sind zehn ________ bei ihr eingezogen, und die sind ________ und laut.
c Vor drei Jahren ist Selma aus der ________ ausgezogen, doch jetzt ist sie wieder zurück. ~~~~~~~~ ist unglücklich, denn Selma wollte schon vor drei Jahren immer die ________ spielen. ~~~~~~~~ konnte und wollte das einfach nicht ________.
d Im Winter musste ~~~~~~~~ immer im Haus bleiben. Er mochte das überhaupt nicht. Jetzt ist es Frühling, und er darf wieder ________ spielen.

2 Markieren Sie in 1 die Präteritum-Formen von den Modalverben *(können, müssen, wollen, dürfen, sollen* und *mögen)* und die Infinitive der anderen Verben.

3 Ergänzen Sie die Präteritum-Formen von den Modalverben. Ergänzen Sie dann die Präsens-Formen.

	Präteritum (früher)	Präsens (jetzt)
ich/er/es/sie (Sg.)/man	konnte, musste, ...	kann, ...
du		
wir/sie (Pl.)/Sie		
ihr		

A2 **4** Präsens oder Präteritum? Lesen Sie die Dialoge und unterstreichen Sie die richtigen Formen.

a ● Mochtest/Magst du Zoos?
■ Früher mag/mochte ich Zoos sehr gern, aber heute tun mir die Tiere leid.
b ● Wir wollen/wollten am Wochenende in den Zoo gehen, komm doch mit!
■ Nein, ich konnte/kann nicht, ich muss/musste nach Hamburg fahren.
c ● Hattest du Zeit? Kannst/Konntest du gestern deine Lieblingsserie sehen?
■ Nein, ich will/wollte sie sehen, aber der Fernseher war kaputt.
d ● Darfst/Durftest du als Kind ein Haustier haben?
■ Ich wollte/will immer ein Haustier haben, aber meine Eltern wollen/wollten das nie.
e ● Warum waren Sie gestern nicht im Büro? Sie sollen/sollten doch die Pläne fertig zeichnen.
■ Ich kann/konnte nicht kommen, ich hatte einen Arzttermin.

Tipp Grammatik
Modalverben im Präteritum stehen meistens mit dem Infinitiv, z. B. *Ich wollte ... füttern.* Vergleichen Sie mit dem Perfekt: *haben/sein* + Partizip II, z. B. *Ich habe ... gefüttert.*

A3 **5** Entschuldigungen. Ordnen Sie zu und ergänzen Sie wie im Beispiel.

(nicht) aufräumen   den Brief (nicht) wegschicken   ~~den Hund (nicht) füttern~~   (nicht) einkaufen   (nicht) zurückrufen

a ● Warum hast du den Hund nicht gefüttert?
■ Ich wollte ihn füttern, aber Rollo wollte nicht ins Haus kommen.
b ● Warum hast du ________?
■ Ich wollte ________, aber ich hatte keine Briefmarke.
c ● Warum ________?
■ Ich ________, aber der Supermarkt war geschlossen.
d ● ________?
■ ________, aber ich konnte das Handy nicht einschalten. Der Akku war leer.
e ● ________?
■ ________, aber ich musste den ganzen Tag im Büro arbeiten.

▶ 118 **6** **Lesen Sie das Interview und ergänzen Sie die richtigen Modalverben im Präteritum. Hören Sie dann und vergleichen Sie.**

- ● (~~wollen~~/können) *Wollten* (a) Sie früher schon Tierpfleger werden, Herr Beckmann?
- ■ Nein, als Kind (dürfen/wollen) ______________ (b) ich Cowboy werden. Tiere waren immer schon interessant für mich.
- ● Hatten Sie viele Haustiere?
- ■ Eigentlich nicht. Ich (wollen/sollen) ______________ (c) immer große Haustiere haben, einen Hund zum Beispiel. Aber unsere Wohnung war klein, da (dürfen/mögen) ______________ (d) man keine großen Haustiere halten. Ich hatte Fische.
- ● Warum (müssen/wollen) ______________ (e) Sie dann als Erwachsener Tierpfleger werden?
- ■ Ich (mögen/sollen) ______________ (f) den Beruf schon immer und ich (können/wollen) ______________ (g) auch immer im Freien arbeiten. Ich (können/müssen) ______________ (h) schon mit 17 Jahren im Zoo anfangen. Aber ich (müssen/mögen) ______________ (i) sehr viel über die Tiere und die Tierpflege lernen. Das war manchmal nicht ganz einfach.

Tierpfleger Daniel Beckmann

A4 **7** **Was sollte Herr Schön gestern tun ☹, was wollte er aber lieber tun ☺? Was meinen Sie? Ergänzen Sie die Smileys und schreiben Sie.**

a	um sechs Uhr aufstehen	☹	bis 9:00 Uhr schlafen	☺
b	spazieren gehen	○	im Büro arbeiten	○
c	den Fernseher reparieren	○	ins Kino gehen	○
d	Lebensmittel einkaufen	○	ein Buch lesen	○
e	Rad fahren	○	im Garten arbeiten	○
f	kochen	○	ins Restaurant gehen	○

a Er sollte um sechs Uhr aufstehen, aber er wollte …

8 **Ergänzen Sie die Modalverben und die Informationen aus der Tabelle.**

	Herr Berger	Frau Schmölzer	Jutta und Thomas
mit zehn Jahren	Clown werden (wollen)	kein Gemüse und keinen Salat (mögen)	Klavier spielen (können)
heute	selbstständig werden (wollen)	kein Fleisch (mögen)	Klavier spielen (nicht mehr können)

a Frau Konrad: Was ______________ Sie mit zehn Jahren ______________, Herr Berger?
Herr Berger: Ich glaube *Clown*. Ja, ich ______________________________.
Jetzt arbeite ich in einer Bank, aber ich ______________________________.

b Frau Schmidt: Essen Sie kein Fleisch, Frau Schmölzer?
Frau Schmölzer: Nein, ich ______________ kein Fleisch. Als Kind ______________ ich kein Gemüse und keinen Salat.

c Jan: ______________ ihr ein Instrument ______________?
Jutta und Thomas: Nein. Mit zehn Jahren ______________ wir ein bisschen Klavier ______________.
Aber wir haben alles vergessen. Heute ______________ wir nicht mehr Klavier ______________.

9 **Früher und heute. Schreiben Sie persönliche Sätze.**

a Was mochten Sie früher (nicht)? Was mögen Sie heute (nicht)?
b Was wollten Sie als Kind (nicht) gern tun? Was wollen Sie heute (nicht) gern tun?
c Was konnten Sie als Kind (nicht)? Was können Sie heute (nicht)?
d Was durften Sie als Kind (nicht)? Was dürfen Sie heute (nicht)?

a Früher mochte ich kein … aber heute mag ich …

B1 ▶ 119 **1 Was wissen Sie noch? Hören Sie noch einmal. Wer sagt was wann? Ordnen Sie zu (A oder B). Ordnen Sie dann die Sätze.**

A Judith Fleischer B Heinrich Winter

a ☐ ___: Warum wollen Sie freinehmen?
b ☐ ___: Sie können Ihren Hund mitbringen.
c 1 _A_: Kann ich morgen freinehmen?
d ☐ ___: Wir müssen morgen die Pläne nach München schicken.
e ☐ ___: Mein Hund kann nicht allein zu Hause bleiben.
f ☐ ___: Können Sie mir nicht einfach frei geben?
g ☐ ___: Warum können Ihre Kinder nicht auf Trixi aufpassen?

2 Schreiben Sie die Sätze aus 1 noch einmal. Schreiben Sie indirekte Fragesätze oder *dass*-Sätze.

1 Judith Fleischer fragt, ob sie am nächsten Tag freinehmen kann.
2 Heinrich Winter will wissen, warum sie ...
3 Judith Fleischer sagt, dass ...

▶ 120 **3 Was wissen Sie noch? Hören Sie noch einmal. Was meinen Sie? Finden Judiths Kolleginnen und Kollegen ein Hundeverbot in der Firma gut / nicht gut? Warum? Ergänzen Sie.**

weil er Angst hat | weil sie eine Hundeallergie hat | weil sie Hunde süß findet

a Robert findet ein Hundeverbot gut, ______________________.
b Helga findet ein Hundeverbot nicht gut, ______________________.
c ______________________, findet Karin ein Hundeverbot sehr gut.

4 Schreiben Sie die Sätze aus 3 in die Tabelle.

	weil-Satz weil		Verb
a Robert findet ein Hundeverbot gut,	weil	er Angst	hat.
b Helga ...			

weil-Satz weil		Verb	
c Weil	sie		findet Karin ...

5 Warum nicht? Finden Sie für jede Frage drei passende Antworten und schreiben Sie *weil*-Sätze.

Sie war krank. | Ich hatte kein Geschenk. | Ich mag die Farbe nicht. | ~~Meine Kinder sind in der Schule.~~ | Ich musste arbeiten. | Ich ziehe lieber einen Pullover an. | Sie musste beruflich ins Ausland fahren. | Mein Mann muss nach Italien fliegen. | Meine Eltern sind im Urlaub. | Ich habe keine Einladung bekommen. | Die Hose ist zu kurz. | Gestern war ein Feiertag.

a Warum kann niemand auf Ihren Hund aufpassen?
b Warum war Ihre Chefin gestern nicht im Büro?
c Warum willst du den Anzug nicht anziehen?
d Warum warst du nicht auf Geralds Geburtstagsparty?

a Weil meine Kinder in der Schule sind. Weil ...

6 Ergänzen Sie *dass* oder *weil*.

a Ich bin sicher, _dass_ wir im Büro nicht rauchen dürfen.
b ________ das Wetter schlecht war, sind wir am Wochenende zu Hause geblieben.
c Mario will heute Abend nicht ausgehen, ________ er seine Lieblingsserie sehen will.
d Marianne hat gesagt, ________ ihre Tante auf ihre Kinder aufpassen kann.
e Carina hofft, ________ sie bei ihrem Gespräch mit der neuen Chefin einen guten Eindruck gemacht hat.
f Ich mag den Käse, ________ er gut riecht und gut schmeckt.

7 **Was wissen Sie noch? Ordnen Sie zu und schreiben Sie *weil*-Sätze.**
Mehr Informationen finden Sie auf den Seiten 72, 78 und 86 im Kursbuch.

a Kevin ist nicht mehr zur Schule gegangen. 3
b Kevin geht heute wieder gern zur Schule. ☐
c Schönheitsoperationen sind in Deutschland sehr beliebt. ☐
d Nach einem Unfall muss man für eine Schönheitsoperation nichts bezahlen. ☐
e Das Internet macht Mobbing für die Täter einfach. ☐
f Frau Peters sieht „Pinguin, Robbe & Co." jede Woche. ☐
g Der Tierpfleger Thomas Dörflein musste Knut mit der Flasche füttern. ☐
h Thomas Dörflein durfte mit Knut bald nicht mehr spielen. ☐

1 Die Eisbärenmutter wollte ihr Kind nach der Geburt nicht annehmen.
2 Die Krankenkasse bezahlt die Arztrechnung nach einem Unfall.
3 ~~Er ist das Opfer von Cyber-Mobbing geworden.~~
4 Sie mag Zoosendungen.
5 Sie können anonym bleiben.
6 Der Eisbär ist schnell groß und gefährlich geworden.
7 Die Schulleiterin konnte eine Lösung finden.
8 Viele Menschen sind mit ihrem Aussehen nicht zufrieden.

a Kevin ist nicht mehr zur Schule gegangen, weil er das Opfer ...
b Kevin ...

8 **Schreiben Sie die Sätze 7b, 8c und 2d aus 7 auch mit *deshalb* wie im Beispiel.**

3a Kevin ist das Opfer von Cyber-Mobbing geworden. Deshalb ist er nicht mehr zur Schule gegangen.
7b Die Schulleiterin ...

B2 **9** **Da stimmt etwas nicht! Tauschen Sie die markierten Wörter und korrigieren Sie so die Fehler.**

a Er will wissen, warum sie ~~der Drucker~~ die Brille vergessen hat.
b Es ist sicher die Batterien kaputt, deshalb funktioniert das Licht nicht.
c Die EC-Karte funktioniert, aber die Heizung ist falsch.
d Das Kabel ist wieder o. k., und ~~die Brille~~ der Drucker funktioniert wieder.
e Es gibt leider keine Fotos, denn kein Papier ist schon voll.
f Weißt du, ob die Birne in der Taschenlampe neu sind?
g Es war nicht der PIN-Code kaputt, sondern das Fenster war offen.
h Ich glaube, dass der CD-Player aus der Steckdose kommt.
i Der Kopierer funktioniert nicht, weil die Speicherkarte mehr da ist.
j Du kannst das Lied auf dem Computer hören oder kein Strom spielt es für dich.

10 **Was passt? Ordnen Sie die Satzteile mit den unterstrichenen Wörtern aus 9 zu.**

1 Konjunktion + Nebensatz / indirekte Frage
a warum sie die Brille ...
...

2 Konjunktion + Aussagesatz
c aber die ...
...

3 Konjunktion + Aussagesatz mit Inversion
b deshalb funktioniert ...
...

Tipp Grammatik
Wörter wie *weil, deshalb* oder *aber* geben dem Satz bestimmte Regeln. Zum Beispiel:
– Nach *weil, dass* usw. steht ein Nebensatz.
– Nach *und, aber, oder* usw. steht ein Aussagesatz.
– Nach *deshalb** steht ein Aussagesatz mit Inversion.
Lernen Sie die Regeln zusammen mit diesen Wörtern.

* *deshalb* kann an verschiedenen Positionen im Satz stehen.

C

C1 ▶ 121 **1 Was wissen Sie noch? Hören Sie noch einmal. Unterstreichen Sie die richtigen Konjuktionen und schreiben Sie die markierten Wörter richtig.**

Seit einigen Jahren leben wieder Wölfe in der Schweiz, denn/aber (a) manche Schweizer sind nicht glücklich. Die Wildtiere ~~örsten~~ stören die Bauern, dass/weil (b) sie eine Gefahr für ihre aSchfe sind. Manche Bauern wollen ihre aSchfe verkaufen. Sie afschlen oft schlecht, denn/weil (c) sie in der Nacht Wölfe hören. Die Tierschützer sind rfho, ob/dass (d) Wölfe über die rnzeGe in die Schweiz kommen. Sie verstehen die Bauern nicht deshalb/und (e) sie sagen: „Vielleicht muss manchmal wirklich ein aSchf sterben, sondern/aber (f) die Bauern bekommen Geld für das Tier. Auch für Schutzhunde gibt es Geld, weil/denn (g) sie sollen auf die aSchfe aufpassen. Die Bauern müssen ein muorFlar ausfüllen und unterschreiben oder/und (h) das Geld für den Hund kommt dann auf ihr Knoot."

2 Bauern oder Naturschützer? Wer sagt was? Ordnen Sie zu (A oder B) und schreiben Sie Sätze wie im Beispiel.

A Bauern B Naturschützer

a A (weil) Die Wölfe müssen weg. Sie können auch für Menschen gefährlich werden.
b ☐ (und) Früher konnten Wölfe in den Alpen gut leben. Auch heute können wir mit ihnen zusammenleben.
c ☐ (dass) Wir sind sicher. Auch die Touristen wollen in der Nacht keine Wölfe hören.
d ☐ (aber) Wölfe sind Wildtiere. Sie sind nicht gefährlich für die Menschen.
e ☐ (ob) Wir wissen am Abend nie: Leben noch alle Tiere am nächsten Tag?
f ☐ (wieso) Wir können nicht verstehen: Wieso kaufen die Bauern keine Hunde?

a Die Wölfe müssen weg, weil ...

C2 **3 Landschaften. Finden Sie die Wörter und ordnen Sie sie den Bildern (a–l) zu. Schreiben Sie auch die Artikel und die Pluralformen.**

MEER|DORFSTADTLANDBERGSTRAND

TALFELDWALDFLUSSSEEAUTOBAHN

a das Meer (-e), ...

▶ 122 **4 Was wissen Sie über die deutschsprachigen Länder? Ergänzen Sie Wörter aus 3 (___) und die Ländernamen Österreich, Deutschland oder Schweiz (___). Hören Sie dann die Lösung.**

a Hamburg ist eine große *Stadt* im Norden von ________.
b Der große ________ an der Grenze zwischen ________, ________ und der ________ heißt Bodensee.
c Die höchsten ________ (Pl.) findet man in den Alpen in ________ und der ________.
d Beliebte ________ (Pl.) gibt es im Norden von ________, zum Beispiel auf der Insel Rügen.
e Die Donau ist der wichtigste ________ im Süden von ________ und in ________.
f Auf den ________ (Pl.) in ________ darf man sehr schnell fahren.

5 Beschreiben Sie Ihr Heimatland. Schreiben Sie mindestens sechs Sätze.

Mein Heimatland ist ...
... ist ... Quadratkilometer groß.
Im Norden/Süden/Osten/Westen gibt es ... Dort gibt es auch ...
In der Mitte ist/sind ...
Die meisten Menschen leben im Norden/Süden/Osten/Westen ...

123-125 **6** Was fehlt? Hören Sie die Beschreibungen zu den Bildern auf Seite 91 im Kursbuch. Was fehlt auf den Bildern?

A

B

C

Auf Bild A fehlen ...

7 Finden Sie acht Tiere und eine Pflanze. Ergänzen Sie die Sätze.

a Vorne *im Schnee* liegt *ein Schaf*.
b Zwischen *dem* ________ und ________ ist ________.
c Links neben ________ sieht man ________.
d Vor ________ ist ________.
e Auf ________ sieht man ________.
f Unter ________ sind ________ und ________.
g Ganz hinten, neben ________ ist ________.
h Über ________ ist ________.
i Zwischen ________ und ________ ist ________.

Aussprache

126 **1** Wo hören Sie ö? Im ersten oder im zweiten Wort? Kreuzen Sie an.

	a	b	c	d	e	f	g	h	i	j
Wort 1:	X									
Wort 2:										

127 **2** Hören Sie und sprechen Sie nach.

können – kennen	sehen – hören	lesen – lösen	höflich – hässlich	böser – besser
könnt – kennt	gehen – schön	Wörter – Wetter	Wölfe – welche	Vögel – Fehler

- Hören Sie bitte. Lesen Sie den Text und lösen Sie dann die Aufgabe. Kennen Sie die Wörter? Können Sie die Wörter lesen?
- Sterne, stören, plötzlich, Söhne, Seen.
- Welche Wörter sind Nomen?

Schreibwerkstatt

1 Lesen Sie die Texte aus den Internet-Tagebüchern. Wie war es früher, wie ist es heute? Machen Sie Notizen.

INTERNET-TAGEBUCH

von: Marianne

22. 5.: Ich habe ein paar Tage frei und bin nach Fischbach gefahren. Wir waren früher immer hier im Urlaub, aber heute ist alles anders. Früher konnten wir in den kleinen Geschäften im Dorf einkaufen. Heute müssen wir zehn Kilometer mit dem Auto fahren, weil es fast keine kleinen Geschäfte mehr im Dorf gibt. Früher durften wir auch in den Wald gehen und spielen. Den Wald gibt es heute nicht mehr. Dort ist jetzt die Autobahn. Aber nicht alles war früher besser. Mit 14 wollte ich oft ausgehen, aber ich durfte nicht. Und heute? ... Heute bin ich oft nicht in Stimmung für die Disco.

Petras Internet Diary

15. 5. Ich habe gerade mit meinem Cousin geskypt. Er ist in China. Eine Stunde lang hat er mir erzählt, wie es ihm dort gefällt. Meine Großmutter hat vor vielen Jahren in den USA studiert. Damals hatte man noch keine Ahnung vom Internet. Man konnte nicht skypen, man musste telefonieren oder Briefe schreiben. Das Telefonieren war sehr, sehr teuer, und ein Brief ist erst nach zehn Tagen angekommen. Es ist soooo gut, dass es Internet gibt.

Jakobs Logbuch

19. 5. Ich habe wieder einmal eingekauft, ... im Internet. Ich mag einfach keine Einkaufszentren und keine großen Geschäfte. Früher musste ich mit meinem Motorrad ins Einkaufszentrum oder in die Stadt fahren. Ich musste wissen, wann und wie lange die Geschäfte geöffnet haben. Ich musste eine Verkäuferin oder einen Verkäufer fragen, oder ich musste alles selbst im Geschäft suchen. Heute kann ich zu Hause sitzen und einkaufen, wann ich will. Es ist einfach so praktisch. ... Nur für mein Konto ist es nicht so gut.

	früher	heute
Marianne	in Fischbach in den kleinen Geschäften ...	
Petra		
Jakob		

2 Was war vor 5, 10, 15 ... Jahren für Sie anders? Sammeln Sie Ideen in der Mindmap.

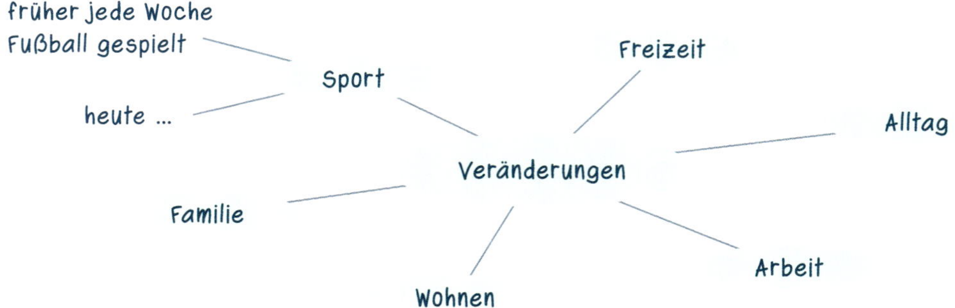

3 Schreiben Sie einen Text für Ihr persönliches Internet-Tagebuch. Was war früher für Sie anders?

Ich bin/habe gerade ...
Vor ... Jahren/früher musste/konnte/durfte/wollte ich ...
Heute/Das ist ...

Tipp Schreiben
Sammeln Sie vor dem Schreiben Ideen. Mindmaps können Ihnen dabei helfen.

→ Hier können Sie weiterlernen: www.hueber.de/motive

Lernwortschatz

Einstiegsseite
die Jahreszeit, -en
der Pilz, -e
A: das Schwammerl, -n
Russland
die Winterkleidung

räumen
sammeln
wegtun

wunderschön

Schnee räumen

A1
das Autodach, ¨-er
die Chemie
das Dach, ¨-er
das Gericht, -e
das Gewitter, -
die Gewitterwolke, -n
der Hagel
das Hausdach, ¨-er
die Hexe, -n
der Himmel, -
das Hühnerei, -er
das Jahrhundert, -e
das Metall, -e
der Rauch
die Richtung, -en
die Technik, -en

blitzen
donnern
klopfen
manipulieren

chemisch
heiß
kühl

damals

A3
die Hitze
die Kälte
der Nebel
der Sturm, ¨-e
die Temperatur, -en
die Wärme
der Wetterbericht, -e

hageln
schneien
stürmen

bewölkt
neblig
sonnig
windig

kaum
minus

B1
der/die Angestellte, -n
der Arbeiter, -
der Durchschnitt
die Ferien (Pl.)
die Planung, -en
die Urlaubsplanung

schließen
verbringen

wenn

B2
die Aktivität, -en
das Chaos
die Eile
der Fingernagel, ¨-
die Grillparty, -s
das Geschirr
die Pizzeria
die Prüfungsfrage, -n

planen
schimpfen
spülen
A: abwaschen
vergessen

ängstlich
tolerant

C1
der Fahrer, -
der Fernfahrer, -
die Fernfahrerin, -nen
der LKW, -s / der Last(kraft)wagen, -
CH *auch*: der Camion, -s
die Ostsee
das PS, -
der Skifahrer, -
der Starkregen
der Stau, -s
die Tonne, -n (t)

schaffen

glatt
verrückt

unterwegs

C2
das Hochwasser
die Hütte, -n
die Nordsee
das Schild, -er
der Schutz
das Skifahren
das Stauschild, -er
die Vorsicht

fallen
wechseln

gesperrt

der Schnee fällt
Schutz suchen
über … fahren
zurück sein

C3
das Gewicht, -e
die Höhe, -n
der Liter, - (l)
die Menge, -n
der Milliliter, - (ml)
der Quadratmeter (m^2)
der Zentimeter, - (cm)

messen

A

A1 **1 Was wissen Sie noch? Lesen Sie noch einmal → KB S. 94, A1b. Ergänzen Sie die Wörter und ordnen Sie zu.**

~~Hexen~~ ungefährlich Wiesen Technik Gericht kühlen Donner

a Vor 300 Jahren glaubten viele Menschen, 3
b Vor einem Gewitter mit ______________, Blitz und Hagel rufen die Wetterexperten Johannes Sailer an,
c Die Menschen wussten damals nicht,
d Hagelkörner sind oft sehr groß und gefährlich,
e Man weiß aber nie genau,
f Die „Wetterhexen" kamen oft vor ______________,

1 weil Felder und ______________ nach einem Gewitter kaputt und die Menschen wütend waren.
2 deshalb kämpft man mit ______________ und Chemie gegen Hagelgewitter.
~~3~~ dass Hexen das Wetter machten.
4 ob man den Hagel wirklich ______________ machen kann.
5 dass es in Europa eine „kleine Eiszeit" mit ______________ Sommern und viel Regen gab.
6 und kurze Zeit später sitzt er in seinem Flugzeug.

2 Unterstreichen Sie in 1 alle Präteritum-Formen und ordnen Sie die Sätze zu.

a im 16. und 17. Jahrhundert: a3
b heute:

A2 **3 Präteritum mit -*t*. Schreiben Sie die Präsens-Formen.**

Präteritum mit -*t*	Präsens	Präteritum mit -*t*	Präsens
a er zeigte	er zeigt	g wir hörten	
b wir lernten		h Pia und Jan kochten	
c sie suchte		i es regnete	
d du wartetest		j ich fragte	
e ihr brauchtet		k Silvia lebte	
f Herr Gutmann bezahlte		l man arbeitete	

4 Ergänzen Sie Verben aus 3 im Präteritum.

a Im 16. Jahrhundert glaubten viele Menschen an Hexen. Deshalb lebten manche Frauen in Angst.
b Wir hatten früher eine kleine Wetterhexe aus Metall auf dem Dach. Sie ______________ uns, aus welcher Richtung der Wind kam.
c Im letzten Sommer gab es viele Gewitter. Johannes Sailer ______________ deshalb sehr oft auch an Wochenenden.
d Nach seinem Flug ______________ Johannes Sailer in seinem Auto auf den Hagel.
e Wenig später ______________ er die Hagelkörner auf seinem Autodach.
f Johannes Sailer ______________ mit 18 Jahren fliegen.

5 Wo findet man wohl diese Sätze? Ordnen Sie zu und unterstreichen Sie das Präteritum. Schreiben Sie dann die Präteritum-Formen und die Infinitive.

A Krimi B Liebesgeschichte C Sportsendung

a A Die Bergers waren im Urlaub, das Haus war leer. Im ersten Stock gab es eine Balkontür. Dort war das Wohnzimmer.
b Sie sahen sich an, … lange, sehr lange. Und dann …
c Es stand schon 0:4 für die Gäste, es sah gar nicht gut für sein Team aus. Doch dann kam das Gewitter.
d Nach dem Spiel sprachen wir mit den beiden Trainern.
e Er lief zum Haus, doch die Polizisten waren schneller. Sie kamen durch den Garten.
f Sie nahm seine Hand: „Es wird alles gut …"
g Er fand das Geld im Schreibtisch.
h Sie aß und trank nichts auf der Party. „Wo war er nur? Warum rief er nicht an?"
i Er schrieb ihr Briefe, jeden Tag. Doch er war nicht sicher, ob sie seine Briefe auch wirklich bekam.
j Er fuhr am Ende einfach nicht schnell genug, so wurde er nur Zweiundzwanzigster.

a waren, war – sein; gab – geben; b sahen … an – …

Tipp Grammatik
Das Präteritum von unregelmäßigen Verben ist anders als der Infinitiv (z. B. *stehen – stand*). Lernen Sie das Präteritum von unregelmäßigen Verben gut (Liste s. www.hueber.de/motive).

6 Früher und heute. Unterstreichen Sie die richtigen Zeitangaben.

a Das Internet gibt es seit 1985 / im Jahr 1985.
b Auch heute / Im 17. Jahrhundert glaubte man an Wetterhexen.
c In den letzten Jahren / Heute kamen immer wieder Wölfe über die Grenze in die Schweiz.
d Vor fünfzehn Jahren / In den nächsten Jahren schrieb man viel weniger SMS.
e Ein Laptop kostete im Jahr 1980 / in fünf Jahren so viel wie ein Auto.
f In den 30er-Jahren / Heute lernt man in den Tanzschulen auch Tango.
g Wir fahren letzten Sommer / nächsten Sommer mit dem Zug nach Paris.
h Das Kleid passte ihr in einer Woche / vor zwei Monaten noch.
i Nächsten Sommer / 2014 gab es in meiner Heimatstadt noch kein Einkaufszentrum.

A3 **7** Zwei Postkarten. Ergänzen Sie. Welche Jahreszeit passt zu den Karten?

Grad ~~sonnig~~ Schneesturm Temperaturen bewölkt Wolken Gewitter
neblig Himmel blitzte windig

a

Hallo ihr,
gestern war es noch warm und sonnig.
Es waren 28 ______. Am Abend
kamen ______ und in der
Nacht gab es dann ein ______.
Es donnerte und ______, und
es regnete sehr stark. Heute ist es kühl und
______. Eigentlich ist es zu
kühl für den August.
Eure Anna

b

Liebe Melita,
gestern konnten wir leider nicht Ski fahren.
Es gab einen ______.
Heute haben wir wunderschönen Neuschnee.
Am Morgen war es ______ und
am Vormittag war es noch ______,
aber jetzt sehen wir den ______ wieder.
Es ist sonnig, aber sehr kalt, minus 15 Grad. Wir
hoffen, die ______ steigen bald.
Liebe Grüße Albert

Jahreszeit: a ...

8 Wie ist das Wetter? Schreiben Sie zu den Nomen Sätze mit *es*.

~~Hitze~~ ~~Schnee~~ Kälte Sonne Wind Nebel Wolken Regen Donner Wärme Blitz Sturm Hagel

Hitze – Es ist heiß. / Schnee – Es schneit. / Kälte ...

▶ 128–129 **9** Hören Sie zwei Wetterberichte.
Wie ist das Wetter heute, wie wird das Wetter morgen? Notieren Sie.

Wetterbericht	heute	morgen
a Innsbruck	sonnig, 22°	
b Hamburg		

Tipp Hören
Lesen Sie die Aufgabe ganz genau. Die Aufgabe zeigt Ihnen, was das Thema im Hörtext ist. Wichtige Wörter sind z. B. *Wetter*, *heute* und *morgen*. Passen Sie besonders gut auf, wenn Sie diese Wörter im Hörtext hören. Die Information danach brauchen Sie für die Lösung.

10 Am nächsten Tag: Sie sind in einem Ort aus 9 im Urlaub.
Sie schreiben eine kurze E-Mail an eine Freundin. Sie schreiben, wie das Wetter gestern war und wie das Wetter heute ist.

Hallo ...,
Du fragst, wie das Wetter bei uns in ... ist.
Heute regnet es / scheint die Sonne / ... und ...
Gestern war das Wetter besser / schlechter.
Es waren ... Am Morgen / Am Abend ...
Ich hoffe, bei Euch ist das Wetter besser / auch so gut / ...
Viele / Liebe Grüße ...

B

B1 **1 Lesen Sie den Text zu Fabiane Winklers Urlaubs- und Arbeitszeiten und ergänzen Sie.**

Wetter nehme Urlaub zu Hause ~~Angestellte~~ Hotel
Sehenswürdigkeiten Durchschnitt

Angestellte (a) haben in Deutschland im __________ (b) 30 Tage Urlaub im Jahr. Ich kann also sechs Wochen im Jahr __________ (c) nehmen. Meistens __________ (d) ich im Winter ein paar Wochen frei, denn im Winter gibt es für mich nicht so viel Arbeit. In meinem Beruf muss ich viel reisen. Ich schlafe jede Nacht in einem anderen __________ (e). Am Tag fahre ich dann von einer Stadt zur anderen und zeige unseren Kunden __________ (f). Deshalb bleibe ich in meinem Urlaub am liebsten __________ (g). Da ist mir dann auch das __________ (h) egal. Ich brauche nur Zeit für mich und ein paar gute Bücher.

Fabiane Winkler, Reiseleiterin

2 Wie ist es bei Ihnen? Schreiben Sie fünf persönliche Sätze.

Ich habe ... Tage / Wochen / ... im Jahr Urlaub / Ferien.
Ich nehme / mache immer im Sommer / Winter / ... Urlaub.
Ich bleibe am liebsten ...
Ich fahre (gern) nach ...
... ist mir egal. Für mich ist ... wichtig / am wichtigsten.

▶ 130 **3 Was wissen Sie noch? Hören Sie noch einmal. Lesen Sie die Sätze und kreuzen Sie an.**

a Simon
☐ möchte die Urlaubsplanung machen.
☐ mit Bettina Urlaub machen.
☐ im Sommer arbeiten.

b Wenn es im August regnet, möchte Bettina
☐ den Sommer im Süden verbringen.
☐ lieber arbeiten.
☐ die Firma schließen.

c Wenn das Wetter im September schön ist, möchte Bettina
☐ Ski fahren. ☐ arbeiten. ☐ wandern gehen.

d Bettina will
☐ im August ☐ im Winter ☐ im Herbst
Urlaub nehmen, weil es im Winter vielleicht wieder keinen Schnee gibt.

e Bettina kann keinen Urlaub nehmen, weil
☐ Simon dann böse wird.
☐ sie ihren Urlaub für dieses Jahr schon genommen hat.
☐ die Chefin die Firma schließen will.

4 Alte Wetterregeln aus Bayern und Österreich. Schreiben Sie die Regeln richtig.

a stürmt und schneit / es / Wenn / am 2. 2. (zu „Lichtmess“ = 40 Tage nach Weihnachten) /, // ist der Frühling nicht mehr weit.
b es / Wenn / regnet / am 14. 2. (zu „Valentin“) /, // regnet es den ganzen Frühling.
c es / im März Schnee / gibt / Wenn /, // ist das für die Felder schlecht.
d im Mai / es / Wenn / regnet /, // ist das für die Felder gut.
e Wenn es im Juli heiß ist, // der September / sonnig und warm / wird /.
f ist / es / im November / Wenn / kalt /, // gibt es einen langen und kalten Winter.

a Wenn es ...

5 Lesen Sie die Regeln aus 4 noch einmal. Was meinen Sie?
Welches Wetter wünschen sich die Bauern? Schreiben Sie Sätze wie im Beispiel.

a Die Bauern möchten, dass es am 2. 2. stürmt und schneit. b ...

6 Ordnen Sie zu und finden Sie so Regeln für den Alltag, im Büro und für den Straßenverkehr.

a Wenn man mit dem Fahrrad in der Nacht fährt, [4]
b Wenn man krank ist, [ ]
c Wenn Kollegen oder Kolleginnen Geburtstag haben, [ ]
d Wenn die Ampel Rot zeigt, [ ]
e Wenn man Auto fährt, [ ]
f Wenn mehrere Kollegen in einem Büro arbeiten, [ ]
g Wenn man mit dem Fahrrad nach rechts oder links fahren will, [ ]
h Wenn man Urlaub machen möchte, [ ]

1 darf man dort keine laute Musik spielen.
2 soll man alles Gute wünschen.
3 muss man die Chefin oder den Chef fragen.
4 ~~muss man ein Licht am Fahrrad haben.~~
5 darf man den Führerschein nicht zu Hause vergessen.
6 muss man stehen bleiben.
7 muss man im Büro anrufen oder eine E-Mail schreiben.
8 muss man ein Handzeichen geben.

B2 **7** Gemeinsame Aktivitäten planen, Teil 1: Es gibt ein Problem.
Ordnen Sie zu und schreiben Sie Dialoge wie im Beispiel.

a einkaufen gehen — 4
b wandern gehen
c neue Möbel kaufen
d Campingurlaub machen
e zum Rockkonzert gehen

1 viele alte Möbel haben
2 es regnet sicher
3 zu laut sein
4 ~~kein Geld auf dem Konto haben~~
5 kein Zelt haben

a ∘ Gehen wir gemeinsam einkaufen?
△ Nein danke, ich habe kein Geld ...
b ∘ Sollen wir am Wochenende gemeinsam wandern gehen?
△ Lieber nicht, es ...

8 Gemeinsame Aktivitäten planen, Teil 2: Problemlösung. Lesen Sie das Beispiel.
Finden Sie dann ein Ende zu Ihren Dialogen aus 7 und schreiben Sie Sätze mit *wenn*.

~~mit Kreditkarte bezahlen → etwas kaufen können~~ ganz hinten einen Platz suchen → es nicht so laut sein
jemandem die alten Möbel schenken → wieder Platz haben in den Süden fahren → wahrscheinlich die Sonne sehen
ein Zelt auf dem Campingplatz mieten → Campingurlaub machen können

a ∘ Gehen wir gemeinsam einkaufen?
△ Nein danke, ich habe kein Geld auf dem Konto.
∘ Wenn wir mit Kreditkarte bezahlen, können wir schon etwas kaufen.
△ Du hast recht.

B3 **9** Wen stört was? Schreiben Sie für jede Person zwei Sätze.

a ~~jeden Samstag im Kaufhaus arbeiten müssen~~
b die Geschäfte beim Bezahlen keine Kreditkarten akzeptieren
c die Angestellten zu lange Mittagspausen machen
d der Chef nicht tolerant sein
e die Angestellten nicht pünktlich kommen
f kein Verkäufer Zeit haben

Verkäufer: *Es stört mich, wenn ich jeden Samstag im Kaufhaus arbeiten muss.*
Kunde: ______
Chef: ______

10 Was stört Sie? Schreiben Sie fünf persönliche Sätze.

Es stört mich, wenn meine Chefin / mein Chef / meine Freundin / mein Freund / das Wetter / der Deutschkurs / jemand / ...

C1 **1** Was wissen Sie noch? Lesen Sie noch einmal → KB S. 98, C1a und korrigieren Sie die Fehler im Text.

Anita Pöschl mag ihren Beruf. Es gibt ~~viele~~ nicht viele Frauen unter den Fernfahrern. Anita Pöschl ist oft 240 Stunden im Monat unterwegs. Ihre Freunde und ihre Familie stört das aber nicht. Ihr LKW hat fast 400 PS. Mit ihm fährt sie durch ganz Deutschland, aber nur im Frühling und im Herbst. Deutschland mag sie sehr. Im Sommer macht sie oft mit ihrer Familie in einer schönen Stadt Urlaub. Mit dem Wetter hat Anita Pöschl manchmal Probleme. Glatte Straßen, Gewitter und Starkregen mag sie überhaupt nicht, denn dann ist Chaos auf den Straßen und alles steht im Stau. Anita Pöschl weiß dann, sie schafft es dann erst am Wochenende nach Hause.

C2 **2** *Nach*, *in* oder *zum*? Wann nimmt Anita Pöschl den kleinen LKW, wann nimmt sie den großen LKW? Schreiben Sie Sätze wie im Beispiel.

a (zu) Bahnhof (9 t)
b (zu) Post (7 t)
c (zu) Flughafen (6 t)
d (nach) Italien (17 t)
e (nach) Zürich (20 t)
f (in) Türkei (10 t)

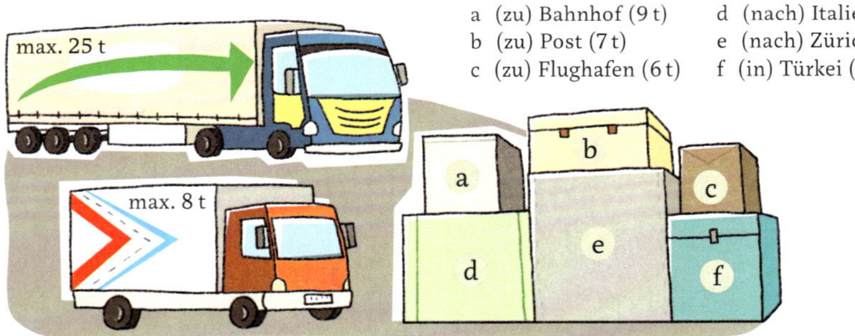

a Wenn Anita Pöschl zum Bahnhof fährt, nimmt sie den großen LKW.
b Wenn sie ...

Tipp Grammatik
Die Präposition *nach* steht vor Ortsnamen ohne Artikel (z. B. *nach Wien, nach Frankreich*), vor Adverbien (z. B. *nach links, nach oben, nach Hause*) und vor Himmelsrichtungen (z. B. *nach Norden**). Die Präposition *in* + Akk. steht vor Ländernamen mit Artikel (z. B. *in die Schweiz, in die Türkei*), vor Nomen mit Artikel steht meist *zu* + Dativ (z. B. *zur Post, zum Bahnhof*).
* = in Richtung Norden

3 Das Wetter in Deutschland. Sehen Sie die Karte an und schreiben Sie Antworten mit Präposition und Dativ.

(an) Meer ~~(in) Alpen~~ (an) Grenze zu Belgien (in) Norden
(an) Bodensee (in) Berge (in) Osten

a Wo schneit es? In den Alpen.
b Wo regnet es? ______
c Wo ist es kalt? ______
d Wo scheint die Sonne? ______
e Wo gibt es Gewitter? ______
f Wo ist es bewölkt? ______
g Wo ist es warm? ______

4 Wir ziehen um! Wo leben die Personen, wohin wollen sie umziehen? Ergänzen Sie die Artikel.

	Familie Henningsen	Frau Walters	Herr Wagner	Sora
	• Norden → • Süden	• Zentrum von Berlin → • Meer	• Stadt → • Nordsee	• Osterseen → • Berge
... wohnt (Wo? + Dat.)	im Norden.	______ Zentrum von Berlin.	in ______ Stadt.	an ______ Osterseen.
... möchte (Wohin? + Akk.)	in ______ Süden.	ans (= an + das) Meer.	an ______ Nordsee.	in ______ Berge.
	maskulin	neutral	feminin	Plural

Tipp Grammatik
Manchmal bilden die Präposition und der Artikel ein Wort, z. B.: *in + dem = im, in + das = ins, an + dem = am, an + das = ans, zu + dem = zum, zu + der = zur, bei + dem = beim, von + dem = vom*

5 Ergänzen Sie.

(an) Bodensee (an) Meer (in) Garten (in) Berge ~~(in) Stadt~~ (in) Stadtzentrum

a Herr Glück hat einen Bauernhof auf dem Land, aber er würde gern _in die Stadt_ ziehen.
b Der Urlaub in den Bergen war schön, aber nächstes Jahr würden wir gern ______ fahren.
c Ich bin im Juli in der Schweiz. Dort würde ich gern ______ fahren und wandern.
d Wenn Sie die Sehenswürdigkeiten sehen wollen, dann müssen Sie ______ gehen.
e Das Meer ist sehr weit weg, aber ihr könnt ______ fahren und dort surfen.
f Warum sitzt du im Zimmer? Geh doch ______, das Wetter ist heute so schön.

6 Möbeltransport. Was kommt wohin?

a _Der Schrank kommt ins Hotel Leopold, ins Restaurant._
b _Das Sofa ..._

7 Ergänzen Sie.

(an) Tür (in) Berge (an) Meer (an) Tisch (in) Stadt (in) Kino ~~(an) Wand~~

a
- Wohin sollen wir das Poster hängen?
- Gleich hier _an die Wand_. Da passt es gut, glaube ich.

b
- Es regnet. Was machen wir heute Nachmittag?
- Gehen wir doch ______. Ich möchte gern einen Krimi sehen.

c
- Ich muss am Nachmittag einkaufen.
- Fährst du ______? Nimmst du mich mit?

d
- Verbringt ihr diesen Sommer wieder am Meer?
- Nein, wir fahren nicht ______, dieses Mal fahren wir ______.

e
- Wohin kommen die Stühle?
- ______ im Wohnzimmer.

f
- Du wolltest doch Elga besuchen.
- Ja, ich wollte sie besuchen. Ich habe auch ______ geklopft, aber es war niemand zu Hause.

Aussprache

▶ 131–132 **1** Hören Sie und sprechen Sie nach.

a am Mittwoch im März
Wie ist das Wetter?
Am Morgen war es neblig.
Jetzt scheint die Sonne.
Kommst du mit dem Bus oder nimmst du ein Taxi?

b im ? April
am Wochen ? ende
um ? elf
am ? ersten ? achten
Lotte ? und ? Otto fahren ? in die Berge.
Am ? Abend ? ist ? es kühl.

▶ 133 **2** Hören Sie und ergänzen Sie ‿ oder **?**. Hören Sie dann noch einmal und sprechen Sie nach.

Hast‿du am Mittwoch Zeit?
Im August haben wir acht Tage Urlaub.
Wie oft hast du frei?
Wie ist das Wetter im Mai?

Schreibwerkstatt

1 **Lesen Sie die E-Mail. Welche Pläne haben Gudrun und Bernd für den Sommer? Welche Ideen hat Gudrun? Unterstreichen Sie sie in der E-Mail.**

Lieber Bernd,

ich finde es toll, dass unsere Familien im Sommer gemeinsam Urlaub machen wollen. Günter und ich haben schon ein paar mögliche Urlaubsorte für uns gefunden. Wir können zum Beispiel ans Meer fahren. In Italien gibt es sehr schöne Strände. Wir können aber auch in den Bergen Urlaub machen. Zwei Wochen wandern und Pilze suchen ist vielleicht auch sehr nett. Sollen wir ans Meer oder in die Berge fahren? Was meinst Du?

Liebe Grüße
Gudrun

2 **Bernd ist ein Pessimist. Welche Probleme sieht er bei einem Urlaub am Meer, welche Probleme sieht er bei einem Urlaub in den Bergen? Schreiben Sie die Probleme in die Tabelle.**

Hallo Gudrun,

vielen Dank für Deine E-Mail. Ich weiß nicht, ob ein Italienurlaub eine gute Idee ist. Wenn das Wetter schlecht ist, kann man nicht an den Strand gehen. Wenn es aber sehr heiß ist, muss man im Appartement Schutz suchen. Wenn zu viele Leute am Strand sind, findet man dort keine Ruhe. Und wenn das Hotel in einer lauten Straße liegt, kann man in der Nacht nicht schlafen. Vielleicht ist ein Urlaub in den Bergen doch die bessere Idee. Aber manchmal wird es in den Bergen sehr kühl, auch im Sommer. Und wenn das Wetter verrücktspielt und wenn viel Regen fällt, will man gar nicht gern wandern gehen. Auch Gewitter können in den Bergen sehr gefährlich werden. Pilze suchen macht sicher Spaß. Wenn man aber falsche Pilze findet und isst, kann das gefährlich sein. Dann muss man schnell ins Krankenhaus. Vielleicht haben wir ja noch eine bessere Idee für den gemeinsamen Urlaub.

Viele Grüße
Bernd

Urlaub am Meer	Urlaub in den Bergen
Wetter schlecht → Man kann nicht ...	

3 **Wählen Sie a, b, c oder d aus und sammeln Sie möglichst viele pessimistische aber auch optimistische Argumente zu den Möglichkeiten.**

a Sollen wir im Ausland oder zu Hause Urlaub machen? Sollen wir mit dem Auto oder mit dem Zug fahren oder sollen wir fliegen?

b Sollen wir im Restaurant essen oder selbst kochen? Sollen wir in die Pizzeria oder ins Chinarestaurant gehen?

c Sollen wir eine Wohnung oder ein Haus suchen? Sollen wir die Wohnung oder das Haus kaufen oder mieten?

d Soll ich mit meinem Husten arbeiten gehen oder zu Hause bleiben? Soll ich einfach nur Tee trinken oder zum Arzt gehen?

4 **Sind Sie Optimist oder Pessimist? Ein Freund oder eine Freundin hat Ihnen eine E-Mail mit Fragen aus 3 (a, b, c oder d) geschrieben. Schreiben Sie eine Antwort-E-Mail mit Ihren Argumenten.**

Liebe/Lieber ...,
Du fragst, ob ...
Ich weiß nicht, ob ... eine gute Idee ist.
Ich finde, dass ... eine/keine gute Idee ist.
Wenn man ..., muss man ...
... ist vielleicht zu unpraktisch / zu viel Arbeit / ...
... ist sicher toll/interessant/...
Wenn wir ..., können wir ...
Ich finde, wir ...
Viele/Liebe Grüße ...

→ Hier können Sie weiterlernen: www.hueber.de/motive

Was würdest du jetzt gern machen? 13

Lernwortschatz

Einstiegsseite

die Lebens-situation, -en
das Praktikum, Praktika

ziehen

nass

eigen-
Lehrer werden
in die Stadt ziehen
sonst

A1

die Aushilfe, -n
der Braten, -
der Feierabend, -e
die Fischkarte
der Jazzclub, -s
die Karte, -n
das Menü, -s
die Portion, -en
das Rind, -er
der Rinderbraten, -
A/CH: der Rindsbraten, -
das Rindfleisch
der Schluss
die Verabredung, -en

aus sein
Schluss machen

A2

das Besteck, -e
der Essig
die Gabel, -n
der Gegenstand, ¨-e
das Geldstück, -e
das Glas, ¨-er
der Löffel, -
das Messer, -
das Öl
der Pfeffer
das Salz
der Schmuck
die Serviette, -n
der Teller, -

fehlen

A3

die Nachspeise, -n
CH: das Dessert, -s
der Spaziergang, ¨-e
der Stadtpark, -s
die Vermutung, -en

schade

B1

der Autositz, -e
die Garderobe, -n
der Gedanke, -n
die Hosentasche, -n
der Schreibtisch, -e

behalten
hängen
klappen
legen
merken
stecken

peinlich
unangenehm
wunderbar

öfter

B2

die Garage, -n
der Sitz, -e

stellen

B3

die Coladose, -n
die Decke, -n
die Dose, -n
die Garage, -n
die Kaffeetasse, -n
der Kamm, ¨-e
die Kanne, -n
CH: der Krug, ¨-e
die Kette, -n
der Spiegel, -
die Tasse, -n
A: das Haferl/Häferl, -n
die Teekanne, -n

früh aufstehen

C1

die Anzeige, -n
der Beitrag, ¨-e
das Bücherregal, -e
der Installateur, -e
die Jobanzeige, -n
der Keller, -
das Kinderzimmer, -
der Küchentisch, -e
der Maler, -
der Raum, ¨-e
die Soße, -n
die Spüle, -n
A: die Abwasch, ¨-en
CH: das Spülbecken, -
die Terrasse, -n
die Wirklichkeit
die Zimmerdecke, -n

einbauen
streichen
umbauen
umräumen
verändern (sich)
verschieben
zusammenziehen

hellblau
hellgrün
kreativ

Lust haben
prima
ständig

C2

putzen
schneiden

C3

das Computer-programm, -e
das Programm, -e

installieren
lassen

A

A1 **1** **Was wissen Sie noch? Hören Sie noch einmal. Ergänzen Sie die Namen und ordnen Sie zu. Achtung: Zwei Sätze (1–6) passen nicht.**
▶ 134

Andy (Koch) Uschi (Kellnerin) Cornelia (Aushilfe)

a Uschi würde gern den Gästen das Essen bringen.
b ______ würde gern Feierabend machen.
c ______ wäre auch gern im Jazzclub.
d ______ hätte gern frei.

1 Aber Andy will ihr gar nicht zuhören.
2 Aber das geht nicht. Die Gäste sind wichtiger.
3 Aber das Menü ist aus.
4 Aber Andy braucht sie.
5 Aber er hat eine Verabredung.
6 ~~Aber die Speisen sind noch nicht fertig.~~

2 **Unterstreichen Sie in 1 die Konjunktive. Ergänzen Sie dann die richtigen Formen in der Tabelle.**

Konjunktiv II (Wünsche)

	sein	haben	würd- + machen/gehen/arbeiten/…
ich/er/es/sie (Sg.)	wäre gern	______ gern	würde gern machen
du	______ gern	______ gern	______ gern machen
wir/sie (Pl.)/Sie	______ gern	______ gern	______ gern machen
ihr	______ gern	______ gern	______ gern machen

A2 **3** **Schreiben Sie die Wörter mit Artikel und Plural und ordnen Sie sie den Bildern zu.**

azSl ~~vieerStte~~ elöffL lÖ steBeck alGs sseMer igssE ereTll abGel eferfPf

a die Serviette, -n
b …

▶ 135-138 **4** **Was hätten die Personen gern? Hören Sie und ordnen Sie die Wörter (1–10) den Situationen (a–d) zu. Schreiben Sie dann Sätze. Achten Sie auf die richtigen Artikel.**

1 Schokoladenkuchen 2 Pfeffer 3 Hamburger mit Pommes frites
4 Serviette 5 Kaffee 6 Stück Brot 7 Fisch und Salat
8 Portion Rinderbraten 9 Gläser und Besteck 10 Glas Wasser

a 7, … b ______ c ______ d ______

a Die Frau hätte gern …
Der Mann … Sie …
b Der Mann …
und er …
c Die Mutter …
Der Vater …
d Die Frau …
und …

A3 **5 Die Personen haben viele Wünsche. Unterstreichen Sie die richtigen Formen.**

a Herr Kraus (72) würde/hätte/wäre gern surfen lernen. Deshalb würde/hätte/wäre er gern jünger.
b Herr Braun wäre/würde/hätte lieber in einem kleinen Haus am Meer als in einem Hochhaus in Berlin leben.
c Finn wäre/würde/hätte lieber einen Ferrari als einen VW Golf.
d Frau Möller hätte/wäre/würde lieber mit Menschen als am Computer arbeiten.
e Leonie wäre/hätte/würde gern pünktlicher. Sie würde/hätte/wäre gern weniger Streit mit ihrer Chefin.
f Maximilian wäre/hätte/würde gern Tanjas Telefonnummer. Er hätte/wäre/würde gern mit ihr ins Kino gehen.

6 Was wissen Sie jetzt über die Personen in 6? Schreiben Sie Sätze wie im Beispiel.

a Herr Kraus kann nicht surfen. b Herr Braun ...

7 Welche Wünsche haben die Personen? Ordnen Sie zu und schreiben Sie Sätze im Konjunktiv II.

mitspielen | eine größere Wohnung haben | Eintrittskarten haben
in den Bergen sein | schönen Schmuck haben | ein Fahrrad haben

a

Frau Fuchs

b
Sabine

c

Herr Fischer

d

Frau Ernst

e

Herr und Frau Geller

f

Irina

a Frau Fuchs hätte gern ...

8 Was ... hat will ... auch haben. Was ... kann will ... auch können. Schreiben Sie Sätze wie im Beispiel.

a Markos Freund hat einen Porsche. Marko hätte auch gern einen Porsche.
b Frau Bergers Freundin spielt sehr gut Klavier. Frau Berger würde auch ...
c Marlenes Freundin ist eine gute Tänzerin. Marlene ...
d Frau Hoffmanns Freunde haben ein Haus am Meer. ______
e Renés Schwester studiert in Berlin. ______
f Gabis Bekannte ist Lehrerin von Beruf. ______

9 Was hat ...? Was hätten Sie auch gern? Was kann ...? Was würden Sie auch gern können? Vergleichen Sie sich mit anderen Personen und schreiben Sie acht persönliche Sätze.

Mein Bruder spielt sehr gut Fußball. Ich würde auch gern ...
Meine Freundin hat ...

B

B1 **1 Was wissen Sie noch? Lesen Sie noch einmal** → KB S. 104, B1b**. Ordnen Sie zu und ergänzen Sie.**

~~Kopf~~ Jacke merken wiederholen Garderobe Brieftasche Rechnung Beifahrersitz

a Welche peinliche Situation muss Georg im Restaurant lösen? 4
b Wo sucht er seine Brieftasche?
c Wo ist sie vielleicht?
d Warum kann Vergessen gut sein?
e Wann behalten wir Informationen gut?

1 Unser Kopf muss für neue Informationen frei sein.
2 Er sucht sie in seiner __________ an der __________.
3 Wir __________ uns Informationen, wenn wir sie oft __________ und wenn Gefühle dabei wichtig sind.
4 Er kann die __________ nicht bezahlen, weil er seine __________ nicht findet.
5 Er hat sie vielleicht auf den __________ gelegt.

B2 **2 Schreiben Sie die neun Wechselpräpositionen an die richtige Stelle in der Zahl neun.**

in auf über ~~an~~ unter zwischen vor neben hinter

an

3 Wo ist der Ball? Zeichnen Sie ihn an die richtige Position.

a in
b über
c auf
d neben
e hinter
f vor
g an
h unter
i zwischen

B3 **4 Sehen Sie die Bilder an. Schreiben Sie die Nomen richtig und schreiben Sie Sätze.**

a Die oeDs __________ steht im __________.
b Der amKm __________ liegt __________.
c Die nneKa __________ steht __________.
d Die Kttee __________ liegt __________.
e Der eielSgp __________ hängt __________.
f Die aeTss __________ steht __________.

5 Margit sucht ihre Kette. Wohin hat sie ihren Schmuck gelegt? Was sind Margits Gedanken? Schreiben Sie.

a Habe ich sie auf ______ Sofa gelegt?
b Habe ich sie in ______ Tasche gesteckt?
c Habe ich sie an ______ Garderobe gehängt?
d Habe ich sie neben ______ Lampe gelegt?
e Habe ich sie zwischen ______ Zeitungen gesteckt?
f Habe ich sie vor ______ Fernseher gelegt?

Tipp Grammatik
Wo?
→ Wechselpräposition + Dativ
nach: *sein, liegen, stehen, bleiben, …*
Wohin?
→ Wechselpräposition + Akkusativ
nach: *legen, stellen, stecken, …*

▶ 139 **6** **Hören Sie. Manola ist auf dem Weg zum Deutschkurs. Sie beschreibt einige Gegenstände. Was sieht sie wo? Ergänzen Sie, ordnen Sie zu und schreiben Sie Sätze wie im Beispiel.**

Wo?	Gegenstand
a _an der_ Bushaltestelle	1 zwei Weinflaschen
b ______ Haustür	2 Julias Tasche
c ______ Flur	3 ~~Rucksack~~
d ______ Tisch	4 Wintermantel
e ______ Stuhl	5 Radiergummi und Bleistift

a An der Bushaltestelle liegt ein Rucksack. b Neben …

▶ 139 **7** **Hören Sie noch einmal. Wohin haben die Personen die Gegenstände aus 6 gestellt/gelegt/gehängt? Ergänzen Sie und schreiben Sie dann Sätze zu den Situationen in 6 (a–e) wie im Beispiel.**

neben ______ Haustür auf _die_ Bank auf ______ Stuhl
an ______ Garderobe auf ______ Deutschbuch

a Jemand hat den Rucksack auf die Bank gelegt.
b Jemand … c Jemand … d Manola … e Julia …

8 **Beschreiben Sie fünf Gegenstände in Ihrem Haus / Ihrer Wohnung / Ihrem Büro / … Wo ist …? Wohin haben Sie … gestellt/gelegt/gehängt? Schreiben Sie persönliche Sätze wie im Beispiel.**

In meinem Regal liegt eine DVD. Ich habe den Film gestern angesehen und die DVD danach in mein Regal gestellt.

9 **Ordnen Sie zu. Schreiben Sie dann sechs weitere Ausdrücke zu *wo?* und *wohin?* in die Tabelle.**

~~auf den Tisch legen~~ ~~im Regal stehen~~ auf dem Stuhl sitzen an der Decke hängen unter dem Schrank liegen in der Cafeteria essen ans Meer fahren in die Stadt gehen im Bett bleiben in einem Hochhaus wohnen in die Schweiz fliegen in der Küche sein in die Garage fahren

Wo? (Wechselpräposition + Dativ)	Wohin? (Wechselpräposition + Akkusativ)
im Regal stehen	*auf den Tisch legen*

10 **Suchen und finden. Ergänzen Sie.**

a • Wo ist mein Schlüssel? Er hängt doch immer an _der_ Garderobe.
▪ Ich habe ihn auf ______ Schreibtisch gelegt.

b • Hast du mein Handy gesehen? Ich habe es doch neben ______ Fernseher gelegt.
▪ Ich glaube, es liegt auf ______ Klavier.

c • Das Salz ist nicht (in) ______ Küchenschrank.
▪ Ich habe es schon auf ______ Tisch gestellt.

d • Wo ist nur meine Tasche? Sie steht doch immer neben ______ Haustür.
▪ Du hast sie auf ______ Sofa gelegt. Hier ist sie.

e • Ich suche meine Brille. Habe ich sie vielleicht (in) ______ Regal gelegt.
▪ Nein, sie liegt hier auf ______ Boden, neben ______ Bett.

f • Ich finde meine Kreditkarte nicht. Habe ich sie in ______ Brieftasche gesteckt?
▪ Vielleicht hast du sie in ______ Bank vergessen. Ruf doch mal an.

> **Tipp Grammatik**
> Schreiben Sie Lückensätze für andere Lerner. Tauschen Sie Ihre Sätze und üben Sie.
> z. B.: *Meine Tasche liegt auf ______ Stuhl.*
> *Ich lege das Buch auf ______ Tisch.*

11 **Was suchen Sie oft? Schreiben Sie drei persönliche Sätze wie im Beispiel.**

Ich suche oft … Meistens liegt/steht/hängt … Manchmal lege/stelle/hänge ich …

Ich suche oft meine Brille. Meistens liegt sie auf dem Esstisch.
Manchmal lege ich sie aber auch auf den Fernseher.

C

C1 **1 Was wissen Sie noch? Lesen Sie noch einmal** → KB S. 106, C1a**. Sind die Sätze richtig oder falsch? Korrigieren Sie die falschen Sätze.**

	richtig	falsch
Willis Freundin a ~~Willi~~ räumt ständig die Möbel um.		X
b Willis Wohnzimmer wird hellgrün gestrichen.		
c Willi würde gern etwas in seiner Wohnung verändern.		
d Anne4 meint, dass Willi und seine Freundin zu verschieden sind.		
e Uru würde gern in Willis Wohnung die Möbel umräumen.		
f Leo62 glaubt, dass Susanna unangenehme Dinge auf morgen verschieben möchte.		

2 Ordnen Sie die Bilder den Sätzen zu.

1 
~~2~~ 
3 
4 
5 
6 
7 
8 

a Martin spült das Geschirr. 2
b Frau Hofer putzt die Fenster. ☐
c Das Fahrrad wird repariert. ☐
d Die Fenster werden geputzt. ☐
e Jan und seine Freunde streichen die Garage. ☐
f Das Geschirr wird gespült. ☐
g Der Mechaniker repariert das Fahrrad. ☐
h Die Garage wird gestrichen. ☐

3 Nach dem Umzug. Da stimmt etwas nicht. Sehen Sie den Plan an und schreiben Sie Sätze wie im Beispiel.

a Die Spüle steht im Wohnzimmer, die gehört in die Küche.
b Das Bett steht …
c Der Esstisch …
d Der Kleiderschrank …
e Der Herd …
f Die Stühle …

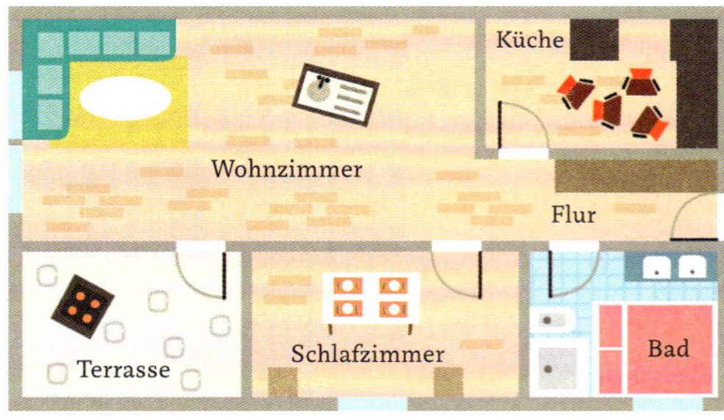

4 Es wird umgeräumt. Was passiert? Schreiben Sie Passivsätze zu den Informationen in 3 wie im Beispiel.

a Die Spüle wird in die Küche gebracht. b Das Bett wird … gebracht. c …

5 Zwei einfache Kochrezepte: Spaghetti und Schinken-Käse-Toast. Ordnen Sie die Satzteile den Rezepten zu und schreiben Sie zwei kurze Texte.

a werden / die Toasts / mit Schinken und Käse / gefüllt / Zuerst /.
b wird / Zuerst / heiß gemacht / Wasser /.
c werden / ins Wasser / die Nudeln / Dann / gegeben /.
d getoastet / die Toasts / Dann / werden / fünf Minuten /.
e werden / Die Nudeln / gekocht / acht Minuten /.
f werden / die Toasts / gestellt / Am Ende / auf den Tisch /.
g wird / gegeben / eine Soße / Zum Schluss / über die Nudeln /.

Spaghetti: Zuerst wird Wasser heiß gemacht. Dann …
Schinken-Käse-Toast: Zuerst …

6 **Jonas kocht Spaghetti, Frau Spät macht Toasts für ihre Kinder. Schreiben Sie die Rezepte aus 5 noch einmal.**

Spaghetti: *Zuerst macht Jonas Wasser heiß. Dann …*
Schinken-Käse-Toast: *Zuerst füllt Frau Spät die Toasts mit Schinken und Käse. Danach …*

C2 7 **Hören Sie den Dialog. Wo ist Herr Schulz?**

▶ 140

Herr Schulz ist …

▶ 140 8 **Hören Sie noch einmal und ergänzen Sie dann das Passiv oder das Perfekt.**

- Wann *wird* das neue Computerprogramm ________? (installieren) (a)
- ▪ Herr Schulz wollte das machen. Aber ich glaube, er ________ das Programm noch nicht ________. (bekommen) (b)
- Sind die Pakete an die Firma Ebner fertig? ________ sie heute Nachmittag pünktlich ________? (wegschicken) (c)
- ▪ Herr Schulz wollte das machen. Aber ich glaube, er ________ die Pakete noch nicht fertig ________. (machen) (d)
- Wann ________ die Räume im Keller ________? (streichen) (e)
- ▪ Herr Schulz wollte die Maler holen. Aber ich glaube, er ________ sie noch nicht ________. (anrufen) (f)
- ________ jemand schon Papier für den Kopierer ________? (bestellen) (g)
- ▪ Das Papier ________ nächste Woche ________. (bringen) (h) Ich ________ es erst heute ________ (bestellen) (i). Herr Schulz wollte das eigentlich machen.
- Und wo ist Herr Schulz? Warum arbeitet er nicht? Er hat wohl keine Lust.
- ▪ Doch, doch. Aber Sie ________ ihn gestern auf eine Dienstreise ________. (schicken) (j)

C3 9 **Ordnen Sie zu und schreiben Sie Sätze mit *lassen*.**

~~Zimmer streichen~~ Fahrrad reparieren Auto waschen Haare schneiden
alle Computerprogramme neu installieren Wohnung jeden Monat putzen

a Marianne gefällt die Farbe in ihrem Wohnzimmer nicht mehr. *Sie lässt das Zimmer streichen.*
b Herr Kuhn hat einen neuen Computer gekauft. *Jetzt lässt er …*
c Herr und Frau Ivancic sind selten in ihrer Ferienwohnung. *Aber sie …*
d Nandors Freundin mag keine langen Haare. *Deshalb lässt er …*
e Kuno mag es nicht, wenn sein Auto schmutzig ist. *Deshalb …*
f Frau Zilk möchte wieder öfter mit dem Fahrrad fahren. *Deshalb …*

Aussprache

▶ 141 1 **Hören Sie. Wo hören Sie i? Im ersten oder im zweiten Wort? Kreuzen Sie an.**

	a	b	c	d	e	f	g	h	i	j
Wort 1:	X	☐	☐	☐	☐	☐	☐	☐	☐	☐
Wort 2:	☐	☐	☐	☐	☐	☐	☐	☐	☐	☐

▶ 142 2 **Hören Sie und sprechen Sie nach.**

spülen – spielen	würde – wird	Tier – Tür	lügen – liegen	viel – Gefühl
vier – für	üben – lieben	ziehen – Züge	fünfzig – vierzig	schließen – Schlüssel

- Wird Ingo fünf?
- ▪ Nein, Ingo wird vier.

- Übt Yvonne gern Klavier?
- ▪ Nein, Yvonne würde lieber mit dir spielen.

- Würdet ihr das Geschirr spülen?
- ▪ Fünfzig Teller für vierzehn Kinder? Das ist viel Geschirr. Habt ihr keine Spülmaschine?

Schreibwerkstatt

1 Lesen Sie den Brief und sehen Sie die beiden Pläne an. Welcher Plan zeigt Daniels wirkliche Wohnung (W), welcher Plan zeigt Daniels Traumwohnung (T)? Ordnen Sie zu.

1 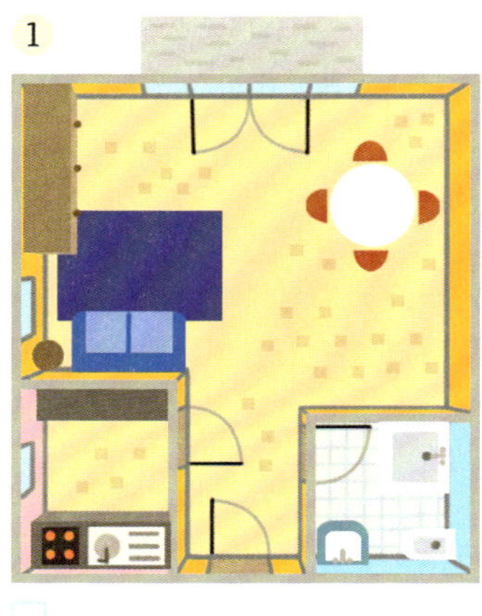

2 

Hallo Petra,

A wie Du weißt, bin ich aus der Wohngemeinschaft ausgezogen. Ich habe jetzt hier in Stuttgart eine eigene Wohnung. Sie ist nicht sehr groß, aber ich bin zufrieden. Die Miete ist nicht sehr hoch, und die Wohnung liegt zentral. Die Wohnung hat eine kleine Küche, ein Bad und ein Wohnzimmer. Das Wohnzimmer hat auch einen kleinen Balkon.

B Im Moment sieht die Wohnung noch nicht so schön aus, aber am Wochenende werden einige Dinge verändert. Zuerst werden die Wände neu gestrichen, die sind im Moment hellblau, rosa und orange. Ich hätte aber gern weiße Wände. Der Schrank wird in den Keller gestellt, und ins Wohnzimmer kommt ein Bücherregal. Das Regal muss ich aber noch kaufen. Ich hätte auch gern ein paar Pflanzen im Wohnzimmer. Die Wohnung ist dann noch nicht perfekt, aber sie gefällt mir dann sicher besser als jetzt.

C Eigentlich hätte ich ja gern eine Wohnung mit einem Schlafzimmer und einer Terrasse. Den Schrank würde ich dann ins Schlafzimmer und nicht in den Keller stellen. Meine Traumwohnung habe ich auch schon gesehen. Sie liegt direkt im Zentrum, nur fünf Minuten von der Universität entfernt. Sie ist prima und ich würde sie gern mieten, aber im Moment ist sie für mich zu teuer. Ich studiere ja noch.

Ich hoffe, Du besuchst mich bald in Stuttgart.

Liebe Grüße
Daniel

2 Lesen Sie den Brief noch einmal und ordnen Sie die Textteile (A, B, C) den Überschriften (1, 2, 3) zu.

1 ☐ Veränderungen in der Wohnung
2 ☐ Daniels Traumwohnung
3 ☐ Daniels neue Wohnung (Lage, Miete, Größe)

3 Schreiben Sie eine E-Mail. Beschreiben Sie Ihre Wohnung. Beschreiben Sie, was Sie in Ihrer Wohnung anders machen möchten und beschreiben Sie Ihre Traumwohnung.

Liebe/Lieber …
ich wohne jetzt schon … Jahre in meiner Wohnung / meinem Haus /…
Ich habe eine neue Wohnung/…
Die Wohnung ist groß/klein/… Sie hat …
Ich würde gern umräumen / etwas verändern …
Am Wochenende / Nächsten Monat … wird/werden … gestrichen/gekauft/weggeräumt/…
… wird ins / in den / in die … geräumt.
Meine Wohnung ist (noch) nicht meine Traumwohnung.
Ich hätte gern … Ich würde gern … Ich wäre gern …
Hoffentlich besuchst Du mich bald.
Viele/Liebe Grüße …

→ Hier können Sie weiterlernen: www.hueber.de/motive

Willst du den Job trotzdem haben? 14

Lernwortschatz

Einstiegsseite
der Artist, -en
der Fensterputzer, -
die Feuerwehr, -en
der Feuerwehrmann, ¨-er
der Flugzeugpilot, -en
der Hubschrauberpilot, -en
der Kinderwunsch, ¨-e
der Pilot, -en
der Tierarzt, ¨-e
der Traum, ¨-e
der Traumberuf, -e

anstrengend
schwierig

trotzdem

A1
die Erfahrung, -en
die Gefahr, -en
die Kenntnisse (Pl.)
der Knochenbruch, ¨-e
die Kurve, -n
die Landung, -en
das Material, Materialien
das Modell, -e
der Notarzt, ¨-e
der Rettungsschirm, -e
der Schirm, -e
der Stein, -e
der Test, -s
der Testflug, ¨-e

bauen
dabeihaben
drehen
feststellen
halten
landen
liefern
probieren
reagieren
testen

hart

obwohl
unten

A2
der Gegensatz, ¨-e

streiten
wechseln

A3
der Platz, ¨-e
die Statistik, -en

A4
der Bauernhof, ¨-e

B1
die Arbeitszeit, -en
das Computersystem, -e
das Gehalt, ¨-er
der Lohn, ¨-e
der Projektmanager, -
die Sekretärin, -nen
der/die Selbstständige, -n
die Software, -s
das Softwaresystem, -e
das System, -e
die Visitenkarte, -n

ausgeben
kündigen
zurückkommen

angestellt
regelmäßig
unregelmäßig

an deiner Stelle

B2
trainieren

B3
das Werkzeug, -e

früh

früh aufstehen

C1
die Ausbildung, -en
die Ausbildungszeit, -en
die Berufsausbildung
der Junge, -n
A: der Bub, -en
der König, -e
das Mädchen, -
der Minister, -
die Pflicht, -en
die Realschule, -n
die Schulpflicht

schicken

durchschnittlich
erwachsen
freiwillig
selbstverständlich
unnötig

eine Ausbildung (zum Friseur/…) machen
A/CH: eine Lehre (zum …) machen
in die Schule schicken

C2
das Abitur
A: die Matura
CH: die Matura / Matur
der Architekt, -en
die Berufsbildende Höhere Schule (BHS) (A)
die Berufsschule, -n
die Gesamtschule, -n
die Grundschule, -n
A: die Volksschule, -n
CH: die Primarschule, -n
das Gymnasium, Gymnasien
CH *auch*: die Kantonsschule, -n
die Hauptschule, -n
der Jurist, -en
der Maurer, -
das Schulsystem, -e

nötig

usw.

C3
das Abendgymnasium, -gymnasien
der Berufswechsel, -

abschließen
nachholen

vermuten

A1 **1** Was wissen Sie noch? Lesen Sie noch einmal → KB S. 110, A1b und ergänzen Sie.

~~Testflüge~~ Stein reagiert Knochenbrüche anstrengend ausprobiert
feststellen Erfahrung Modell Kurven Material

Gleitschirme werden zuerst auf einem Computer getestet. Doch auch _Testflüge_ (a) sind wichtig. Nur in der Luft kann man __________ (b), ob ein Modell richtig __________ (c) und auch wirklich sicher ist. Die Kenntnisse und die __________ (d) von Spitzenpiloten sind da sehr wichtig. Wenn Uli Zenner einen Gleitschirm __________ (e), dann fliegt er mit dem neuen __________ (f) oft bis zu zweihundertmal vom Berg ins Tal. Manchmal testet Uli Zenner am Achensee. Er fliegt gefährliche __________ (g) und dreht den Schirm dabei schnell und immer schneller nach unten. Manchmal hält das __________ (h) nicht, und es gibt eine harte Landung. Uli Zenner fällt dann wie ein __________ (i) ins Wasser. Die Tests sind schwierig, __________ (j) und gefährlich. Bei seinem ersten schweren Unfall hatte Uli Zenner Glück. Die Ärzte stellten mehr als 30 __________ (k) fest, doch ein Jahr später konnte Uli Zenner wieder fliegen.

2 Ergänzen Sie die Präpositionen und die Artikel. Was wissen Sie noch?
Welche drei Informationen stehen nicht im Kursbuch → KB S. 110, A1b ? Kreuzen Sie an.

durch für gegen ohne ohne ~~um~~

Steht nicht im KB.

a Wanderer wandern _um_ (• der) ______ Achensee. ☐
b Die Gleitschirmtests sind ______ (• die) ______ Firmen wichtig. ☐
c Uli Zenner fliegt nie ______ (• sein) ______ Rettungsschirm. ☐
d Bei seinem ersten Unfall ist Uli Zenner ______ (• eine) ______ Bergwand geflogen. ☐
e Von hohen Bergen fliegen Testpiloten oft ______ (• die) ______ Wolken ins Tal. ☐
f ______ (• der) ______ Testflug kann die Firma den Schirm nicht an die Kunden liefern. ☐

Tipp Grammatik
Nach diesen fünf Präpositionen kommt immer der Akkusativ: *durch, für, gegen, ohne, um*

3 Ergänzen Sie *jed-* und die Nomen.

	• der Test	• das Modell	• die Pilotin
Nominativ	jeder Test		
Akkusativ	für	für jedes Modell	für jede Pilotin
Dativ	mit	mit	mit

4 Ergänzen Sie die richtige Form von *jed-*.
Was meinen Sie? Finden Sie die Aussagen richtig oder falsch? Kreuzen Sie an.

	richtig	falsch
a _Jeder_ Chef ist manchmal unangenehm.	☐	☐
b ______ Kind lernt gern.	☐	☐
c In ______ (Dat.) Beruf kann man glücklich sein.	☐	☐
d ______ Frau mag schöne Schuhe.	☐	☐
e ______ Mann gefallen schnelle Autos.	☐	☐
f Mit ______ Haustier kann es Probleme geben.	☐	☐

A2 **5** Finden Sie die Ideen gut ☺, egal 😐 oder nicht gut ☹?
Schreiben Sie die *obwohl*-Sätze richtig und zeichnen Sie Smileys.

a Susanne / hat / Obwohl / Grippe / , // will sie zur Arbeit gehen.
b ganz schrecklich / Mark / singt / Obwohl / , // will er Sänger in einer Rockband werden.
c Herr Kröger will einen Ferrari kaufen, // dann einen Kredit / obwohl / er / braucht / .

d Gerda und Hannes wollen Urlaub auf einem Kreuzfahrtschiff machen, // nicht schwimmen können / obwohl / ihre Kinder /.

e Maria will Auslandsjournalistin werden, // dann auch in gefährlichen Ländern / sie / obwohl / arbeiten muss /.

f Anita will KFZ-Mechanikerin werden, // obwohl / arbeiten / fast nur Männer in dem Beruf /.

a Obwohl Susanne Grippe hat, will ...

6 Ordnen Sie zu und schreiben Sie Sätze mit *obwohl*.

das Fahrrad in der Stadt schneller sein | kein Geld haben | viel Geld verdienen | ~~es regnen~~ | es Sturm geben | in der Schule schlechte Noten haben

a Simon möchte im See schwimmen, obwohl es regnet.
b Herr Seidel möchte ein teures Haus bauen, ______
c Greta und Lilli möchten den Beruf wechseln, ______
d Fabian möchte mit seinem Gleitschirm fliegen, ______
e Lara möchte Medizin studieren, ______
f Herr Schäfer möchte mit dem Auto fahren, ______

7 Was passt: *obwohl* oder *weil*? Unterstreichen Sie.

a Obwohl/<u>Weil</u> Marina erkältet ist, bleibt sie im Bett.
b Max kann nicht Fußball spielen, weil/obwohl sein Bein gebrochen ist.
c Hanna spült das Geschirr mit der Hand, weil/obwohl sie eine Spülmaschine hat.
d Weil/Obwohl Herr Keller seinen Schreibtisch erst gestern aufgeräumt hat, sieht er heute wieder sehr unordentlich aus.
e Weil/Obwohl Manfred jeden Tag mit seinem Chef streitet, will er seinen Job nicht wechseln.
f Frau Schulze kauft das Kleid, weil/obwohl es im Sonderangebot ist.

A3

8 Ergänzen Sie die Sätze an der richtigen Stelle im Text.

Trotzdem kaufte sie für Rex jeden Tag Fleisch ein. **Trotzdem** ging sie mit Rex dort jeden Tag spazieren. **Trotzdem** spielte sie mit ihm jeden Tag Ball. **Trotzdem** liebte Leonore ihn.

Leonore und Rex

Ihre Freundinnen fanden Rex nicht besonders hübsch.
a ______
Leonore mochte den Park am Fluss nicht besonders.
b ______
Ballspiele mochte Leonore eigentlich überhaupt nicht.
c ______
Leonore aß nur Gemüse, weil sie Vegetarierin war.
d ______
Rex war Leonores kleiner Hund aus dem Tierheim, und Leonore liebte ihn einfach über alles.

9 Ergänzen Sie *weil*, *obwohl*, *trotzdem* oder *deshalb*.

a Herr Yilmaz hat sehr lange gearbeitet. trotzdem ist er nicht müde.
Die lange Arbeit stört ihn nicht, ______ er seinen Job mag.
b Petra hat Probleme mit ihrer Chefin, ______ sie oft zu spät zur Arbeit kommt.
______ will sie am Morgen nicht früher aufstehen.
c Gerda mag keine Kühe, Pferde und Schweine. ______ macht sie mit ihrer Familie Urlaub auf dem Bauernhof. Ihre Töchter lieben Tiere. ______ hat sie den Urlaub auf dem Bauernhof gebucht.
d Paul hatte einen Unfall beim Gleitschirmfliegen. Er hatte Glück, ______ der Notarzt sehr schnell an der Unfallstelle war. ______ kann er heute schon wieder mit seinem Gleitschirm fliegen.
e ______ Feuerwehrmann ein gefährlicher Beruf ist, will Kevin Feuerwehrmann werden, ______ auch sein Vater bei der Feuerwehr arbeitet.

B

B1 **1 Traumberufe? Ergänzen Sie.**

als Journalist | in einem Kindergarten | ~~als Tänzerin~~ | bei einer Baufirma | bei der NASA | als Artist

a Irene möchte *als Tänzerin* in der Oper arbeiten.
b Liam möchte als Astronaut ______ arbeiten.
c Jörg möchte ______ bei einer Zeitung arbeiten.
d Pia möchte als Erzieherin ______ arbeiten.
e Ingo möchte ______ in einem Zirkus arbeiten.
f Ralf möchte als Dachdecker ______ arbeiten.

2 Selbstständig oder angestellt? Was passt? Ergänzen Sie.

1 ... bin ich gern selbstständig. **2** ~~... bin ich gern angestellt.~~
3 Ich bin gern selbstständig ... **4** Ich bin gern angestellt ...
5 Deshalb bin ich gern selbstständig. **6** Deshalb bin ich gern angestellt.
7 Trotzdem bin ich gern selbstständig. **8** Trotzdem bin ich gern angestellt.

a Weil ich im Büro wenig Stress habe, *2*
b Obwohl ich wenig Urlaub habe, ______
c ______, weil ich jeden Monat pünktlich mein Gehalt bekomme.
d Mein Gehalt ist nicht sehr hoch. ______
e In der Firma haben wir regelmäßige Arbeitszeiten. ______
f ______, obwohl ich nichts verdiene, wenn ich krank bin.
g Ich bin mein eigener Chef. ______
h Ich muss mir meine Kunden selbst suchen. ______

selbstständig

angestellt

▶ 143 **3 Was wissen Sie noch?
Hören Sie noch einmal und kreuzen Sie an.**

a Volmar erzählt, dass
- ☐ er selbstständig ist.
- ☐ er gekündigt wird.
- ☐ in seiner Firma zwei Angestellte kündigen.

b Er sagt, dass Karina
- ☐ Visitenkarten haben soll.
- ☐ für ihn arbeiten soll.
- ☐ keinen Urlaub nehmen soll.

c Er findet, dass
- ☐ Karinas Lohn sehr hoch ist.
- ☐ die Meinung von Karinas Chef wichtig ist.
- ☐ Karina ihrem Chef die Meinung sagen soll.

d Karina antwortet ihm, dass
- ☐ sie keinen Stress hat.
- ☐ sie Chefin ist.
- ☐ ihr Chef immer schimpft.

**4 Wer sagt das? Welcher Beruf passt? Lesen Sie die Ratschläge und ergänzen Sie die Berufe.
Achtung: Drei Berufe passen nicht.**

Apothekerin | Schneider | Lehrerin | Fensterputzer | ~~Sekretärin~~
Mechaniker | Rezeptionist | Friseur | Köchin

a *Sekretärin*: Wenn ich Sie wäre, würde ich den Chef persönlich fragen, Frau Schröder.
b ______: An Ihrer Stelle würde ich das Auto regelmäßig kontrollieren lassen, Herr Pfeifer.
c ______: An eurer Stelle würde ich die Hausaufgaben gleich nach der Schule machen.
d ______: Sie sollten die Medikamente jeden Tag nehmen.
e ______: Sie könnten die Rechnung für das Zimmer gleich bezahlen.
f ______: Wir sollten mehr vegetarische Speisen auf der Speisekarte haben.

5 Ergänzen Sie die Formen von *sollt-*.

ich	*sollte* ... machen	wir	______ ... machen
du	______ ... machen	ihr	______ ... machen
er/es/sie/man	______ ... machen	sie/Sie	______ ... machen

6 Schreiben Sie die Ratschläge a, b und c aus 4 auch mit *sollt-*.

a Sie sollten den Chef ...

B2 **7** Ordnen Sie zu und geben Sie Ratschläge.

1 Werkzeug kaufen

2 früher ins Bett gehen

3 den Chef fragen

4 ~~zum Zahnarzt gehen~~

5 weniger Geld ausgeben

6 Freunde einladen

a [4] Dominique Huber hat Zahnschmerzen.
b [ ] Martin hat jeden Monat am zwanzigsten kein Geld mehr.
c [ ] Mats ist immer müde.
d [ ] Herr und Frau Lange möchten nicht alleine Silvester feiern.
e [ ] Judith will ihren Hund ins Büro mitbringen.
f [ ] Herr Bauer würde gern sein Fahrrad selbst reparieren.

a Sie sollte zum Zahnarzt gehen. b ...

8 Ordnen Sie zu und ergänzen Sie die Imperative.

kündigen aufstehen anrufen ~~anziehen~~ fahren

a • Uns ist kalt.
▪ Dann _zieht_ eure Mäntel _an_.
b • Ich glaube, Sabrina ist krank.
▪ Na, dann ________ sie doch ______.
c • Ich komme immer zu spät ins Büro.
▪ Dann ________ früher ______.
d • Ich treffe Mario in der Stadt, wir trinken zusammen ein Bier.
▪ Gut, aber ________ nicht mit dem Auto.
e • Wissen Sie, Herr Meier, der Stress in der Firma wird immer stärker.
▪ Dann ________ Sie, Herr Köhler.

9 Schreiben Sie die Sätze aus 8 höflicher. Geben Sie Ratschläge wie in den Beispielen.

a Ihr solltet eure Mäntel anziehen. (An eurer Stelle würde ich die Mäntel anziehen.) b ...

10 Präsens (Ratschlag) oder Präteritum? Kreuzen Sie an.

	Präteritum	Präsens (= Ratschlag)
a Frau Schulze sollte ihre Tochter vom Bahnhof abholen, aber ihr Auto war kaputt.	X	
b Anna sollte mit dem Lernen beginnen. Ihre Prüfung ist nächste Woche.		
c Er sollte seine Freundin anrufen, aber er konnte sein Handy nicht finden.		
d Warum kommen Sie erst um fünf? Sie sollten schon um drei Uhr hier sein.		
e Wir sollten im Sommer zu Hause Urlaub machen. Eine Auslandsreise ist zu teuer.		
f Du solltest öfter trainieren. Wir haben nächsten Monat ein wichtiges Spiel.		

C

C1 **1** **Vor 300 Jahren und heute. Was wissen Sie noch? Lesen Sie noch einmal** → KB S. 114, C1. **Finden Sie neun Wörter. Ergänzen Sie die Sätze und ordnen Sie zu (F = früher/vor 300 Jahren, H = heute).**

MÄDCHENUNNÖTIGKÖNIGDURCHSCHNITTLICHAUSBILDUNGSZEIT

SCHULPFLICHT~~SELBSTVERSTÄNDLICH~~MINDESTENSFREIWILLIG

a Ein Schulbesuch war im 18. Jahrhundert nicht _selbstverständlich_. F
b Kinder müssen ____________ neun Jahre lang in die Schule gehen. ☐
c Der ____________ von Preußen wollte, dass alle Kinder in die Schule gehen. ☐
d Viele Jugendliche gehen oft ____________ länger in die Schule. ☐
e Die Minister fanden die ____________ ____________ und viel zu teuer. ☐
f Man heiratet ____________ acht bis elf Jahre später als früher. ☐
g Die ____________ wird immer länger. ☐
h Die ____________ und Jungen sollten arbeiten und nicht lesen, schreiben und rechnen lernen. ☐

C2 **2** **Ergänzen Sie.**

Gymnasium

Grundschule

Kindergarten

~~Berufsschule~~

Realschule

Hauptschule

Universität

a Die _Berufsschule_ bietet eine spezielle Berufsausbildung.
b Kinder lernen in der ____________ lesen und schreiben.
c Wenn man Arzt werden möchte, muss man an einer ____________ studieren.
d Nach der Grundschule kann man auf eine ____________, eine ____________ oder auf ein ____________ gehen.
e Vor der Schule besuchen viele Kinder einen ____________.

▶ 144–145 **3** **Ausbildung und Beruf. Was passt für die Personen? Hören Sie und ordnen Sie zu.**

Name	Schule Schulabschluss	Berufsausbildung Ausbildung	Beruf Berufswunsch
Dialog 1:	Hauptschule/ Hauptschulabschluss	Universität	Fußballspieler
a Arnold	Realschule/ Realschulabschluss	Fußballtraining	Krankenpflegerin
b Heidi	Gymnasium (Sport- gymnasium)/Abitur	Kurse	Friseur/Visagist
Dialog 2:		Ausbildung und Berufsschule	Journalistin
c Christian			
d Frau Seidel (Oma)			

4 Was war zuerst, was war danach? Schreiben Sie neue Sätze und benutzen Sie die Zeitangaben.

a Ich bin in die Grundschule gegangen. Ich war im Kindergarten. (nach)
b Ich habe die Realschule besucht. Ich habe einen Beruf gelernt. (zuerst … dann)
c Ich habe Abitur gemacht. Ich habe das Gymnasium besucht. (vor)
d Ich habe als Kellnerin gearbeitet. Ich habe die Abendschule besucht. (zur gleichen Zeit)
e Ich habe an der Universität studiert. Ich habe das Gymnasium besucht. (später)
f Ich bin in die Grundschule gegangen. Ich habe die Gesamtschule besucht. (danach)

a *Nach dem Kindergarten bin ich …*

C3 **5** Bernhard Kellers Ausbildung. Welche Antworten passen zu den Fragen? Ergänzen Sie.

Ich bin in die Realschule gegangen. Sechs Jahre. Von 2010–2014. Eine Ausbildung, ich bin Maurer von Beruf. Ich studiere jetzt Bautechnik und ich würde gern nächstes Jahr mein Studium abschließen. Ja, ich bin ins Abendgymnasium gegangen und habe das Abitur gemacht. ~~Ja, drei Jahre lang.~~

a Haben Sie vor der Grundschule den Kindergarten besucht? *Ja, drei Jahre lang.*
b Was haben Sie nach der Grundschule gemacht? ______
c Wie lange dauert die Realschule in Deutschland? ______
d Was haben Sie nach der Realschule gemacht? ______
e Haben Sie nach der Ausbildung zum Maurer noch eine weitere Berufsausbildung gemacht? ______
f Von wann bis wann haben Sie das Abendgymnasium besucht? ______
g Was würden Sie gern in einem Jahr machen? ______

6 Beschreiben Sie die Ausbildung von zwei Personen aus 3.

Arnold ist mit Heidi in den Kindergarten und … gegangen. Danach hat er …

7 Schreiben Sie fünf Sätze über Ihre eigene Ausbildung.

Ich bin (nicht) in den Kindergarten gegangen.
Ich habe von … bis … die Grundschule besucht …

Aussprache

▶ 146 **1** Was hören Sie? Schreiben Sie.

b oder p: p ☐ ☐ ☐ ☐ ☐
d oder t: ☐ ☐ ☐ ☐ ☐ ☐
g oder k: ☐ ☐ ☐ ☐ ☐ ☐

▶ 147 **2** Ergänzen Sie. Hören Sie dann, kontrollieren Sie und sprechen Sie nach.

b oder p:	p lanen	_uch	ein_acken	ge_en	ein _elie_ter _eruf		
d oder t:	scha_e	Ar_ist	mü_e	gla__	_ausend	_assen	_ee
g oder k:	an_estellt	_lopfen	mö_en	_lück	_latt	_ette	Es _ibt _eine _abel.

▶ 148 **3** Was hören Sie, was schreiben Sie? Ergänzen Sie, hören Sie und sprechen Sie nach.

Sie schreiben:	Sie hören:	Sie schreiben:	Sie hören:
Feld	/t/	gel_	/p/
gi_	/p/	Mon_	/t/
ma_	/k/	Umzu_	/k/
Rin_	/t/	blei_	/p/
Stran_	/t/		

Tipp Aussprache
Am Wortende spricht man im Deutschen die Buchstaben *b, d, g* meistens wie *p, t, k.*

▶ 149 **4** Hören Sie und sprechen Sie nach.

Pferd – Pferde
Anzug – Anzüge
Kind – Kinder
Tag – Tage
Kleid – Kleider
anstrengend – anstrengende Tage
gelb – gelbe Kleider

Schreibwerkstatt

1 **Lesen Sie Jasmins E-Mail. Was möchte sie von Lena wissen? Unterstreichen Sie Jasmins Fragen.**

Hallo Lena,

vielen Dank für Deine E-Mail. Ich kann es kaum glauben, dass wir uns 10 Jahre nicht gesehen haben. Schrecklich! Mir geht es gut. Ich arbeite noch immer als Mathematiklehrerin. Unser Markus ist jetzt schon 23 und lebt in Mannheim. Wie geht es eigentlich Deiner Tochter? Vor zehn Jahren war Dora zwölf, heute ist sie erwachsen. Hat sie schon einen Beruf? Macht sie noch eine Ausbildung? Hat sie schon eine Familie? Erzähl doch.

Herzliche Grüße
Jasmin

2 **Lesen Sie Lenas Antwort und ordnen Sie die Fragen (1–4) den Textteilen (A–D) zu.**

1 Wie wichtig sind Beruf und Familie für Lenas Tochter Dora?
2 Was muss Dora in ihrem Beruf tun?
3 Was gefällt ihr (nicht) in ihrem Beruf?
4 Welche Ausbildung hat Dora gemacht?

Liebe Jasmin,

A ☐ vielen Dank für Deine schnelle Antwort. Es ist schön, dass es Dir gut geht. Du fragst, was Dora so macht. Sie ist Krankenschwester von Beruf. Sie hat ein Gymnasium besucht und das Abitur gemacht. Danach ist sie zwei Jahre lang in eine Krankenpflegeschule gegangen. Seit einem Jahr arbeitet sie in einem Krankenhaus.

B ☐ Dort muss sie meistens schon um sechs Uhr am Morgen mit der Arbeit beginnen. Das heißt, sie muss schon um fünf Uhr aufstehen. Manchmal muss sie auch in der Nacht oder am Wochenende arbeiten. Am nächsten Tag hat sie dann aber frei.

C ☐ Obwohl der Beruf sehr anstrengend ist, arbeitet sie gern als Krankenschwester. Sie hat Kontakt mit vielen Menschen, und sie wollte immer schon anderen helfen. Das gefällt ihr. Nur der Arbeitsbeginn um sechs gefällt ihr nicht. Wie Du weißt, hat Dora immer schon gern lang geschlafen. Ich finde, sie sollte einfach früher ins Bett gehen. ;-)

D ☐ Dora hat einen Freund, und sie möchten im Herbst heiraten. Sie möchten später auch Kinder haben, aber jetzt ist der Beruf wichtiger für sie. Ich kann das verstehen. Trotzdem finde ich es schade. Ich hätte gern ein Enkelkind. Was ist denn Dein Markus von Beruf? Gefällt ihm sein Beruf auch? Hat Markus schon Familie? Wie geht es Deinem Mann?

Schreib bald.
Liebe Grüße
Lena

3 **Denken Sie an Verwandte, Freunde oder Bekannte. Schreiben Sie einen Text und beantworten Sie die vier Fragen.**

a Welche Ausbildung hat die Person gemacht?
b Was muss die Person in ihrem Beruf tun?
c Was gefällt ihr (nicht) in ihrem Beruf?
d Wie wichtig sind Beruf und Familie für die Person?

Meine Mutter / Mein Vater /… ist … von Beruf. Sie/Er ist auf … gegangen / hat studiert.
Sie/Er muss jeden Tag …
Obwohl …, gefällt ihr/ihm …
Sie/Er … nicht gern … Trotzdem …
Sie/Er kann … Deshalb …
Sie/Er hat Zeit / keine Zeit für ihre/seine Familie, weil …
Ich finde, sie/er sollte …

→ Hier können Sie weiterlernen: www.hueber.de/motive

Freust du dich auf mich? 15

Lernwortschatz

Einstiegsseite
der Arbeits-
kollege, -n

A1
der Fernsehsender, -
die Fernsehshow, -s
die Fernsehunter-
haltung
der Kandidat, -en
die Kritik, -en
der Lebenspartner, -
der Moment, -e
die Privatsache
das Publikum
die Show, -s
die Szene, -n
der Teilnehmer, -
der Traumpartner, -
der Vertrag, ¨-e

ärgern (sich)
erleben
filmen
freuen (sich)
kümmern (sich)
senden
teilnehmen
vereinbaren
verlieben (sich)
wecken

täglich

außerdem
halb so schlimm

A2
anmelden (sich)
entspannen (sich)
konzentrieren (sich)
umziehen (sich)
unterhalten (sich)
vorbereiten (sich)
vorlesen
wählen

witzig

A3
der Gesprächs-
termin, -e
das Studio, -s
das Treffen, -

beschweren (sich)
bewegen (sich)
duschen (sich)
fühlen (sich)

schwach

B1
das Amt, ¨-er
der Automat, -en
der Beamte, -n
der Enkel, -
die Familien-
ähnlichkeit, -en
die Gebühr, -en
der Glückwunsch, ¨-e
die Papiere (Pl.)
das Passfoto, -s
der Stempel, -
das Unfallkranken-
haus, ¨-er

ablaufen

breit
rund

Herzlichen Glück-
wunsch!

B2
die Geburts-
urkunde, -n
der Kleider-
schrank, ¨-e
der Lichtschalter, -
der Motor, -en
das Motoröl
der Schinken, -
die Schwimm-
brille, -n
der Sonnenschirm, -e
der Topf, ¨-e
CH: die Pfanne, -n
die Überschrift, -en

frisch
hart
reich
reif
scharf
weich

zum Kochen

B3
der Bart, ¨-e

genauso

C1
die Beziehung, -en
die Chance, -n
der Ehepartner, -
die Frauenfreund-
schaft, -en
die Freundschaft, -en
der Gesprächs-
partner, -
die Männerfreund-
schaft, -en
das Telefon-
gespräch, -e
die Umfrage, -n
der Unterschied, -e

aufwecken
sich gehen lassen
nah sein (sich)
wiederentdecken
(sich)

best-
nah

der-/das-/dieselbe

C2
das Moped, -s

C3
die Band, -s
das Einkaufen
die Gewohnheit, -en
das Haustier, -e
das Kennenlernen
die Mutter-
sprache, -n
der Tagesablauf, ¨-e
der Traum, ¨-e

kommentieren
üben

besonder-

A

A1 **1 Was wissen Sie noch? Lesen Sie noch einmal** → KB S. 118, A1b **und ordnen Sie zu.**

a Marina und Jörg haben als Kandidaten
b Deutsche Fernsehzuschauer können
c Für die Fernsehmacher sind Kennenlernshows
d Zwischen den Teilnehmern und dem Fernsehsender wird
e Obwohl die peinlichen Szenen in den Shows

1 immer wieder kritisiert werden,
2 gute Fernsehunterhaltung,
3 an einer Fernsehshow teilgenommen
4 fast täglich erleben,
5 in einem Vertrag vereinbart,

A weil die Sendungen beim Publikum starke Gefühle wecken.
B kümmern sich manche Fernsehmacher nicht um Kritik.
C dass der Sender auch peinliche Szenen senden darf.
D wie sich zwei Menschen im Fernsehen verlieben.
E und sich dort kennengelernt.

2 Ergänzen Sie *manch-* und die Nomen.

	• der Sender	• das Programm	• die Kandidatin	• die Shows
Nominativ	mancher Sender			
Akkusativ	für	für manches Programm	für	für
Dativ	von	von	von mancher Kandidatin	von

Tipp Grammatik
manch- vgl. *der/die/das: mancher* ist ein DER-Wort wie *dieser, welcher, jener* und *jeder*.
Vergleichen Sie: *der Test, mancher Test, dieser Test, welcher Test, jener Test, jeder Test*

3 Was passt? Ergänzen Sie *jed-* oder *manch-*. Alle oder nicht alle? Kreuzen Sie an.

		alle	nicht alle
a	Manche ______ Fernsehsender haben keine Kennenlernshows im Programm. Das sind aber nur wenige.	☐	X
b	______ Fernsehzuschauer finden Kennenlernshows peinlich.	☐	☐
c	______ Kandidat und ______ Kandidatin muss vor der Show einen Vertrag unterschreiben.	☐	☐
d	______ Teilnehmer möchte in der Show seinen Traumpartner finden. Das ist aber nicht möglich.	☐	☐
e	Für ______ Kandidatin und für ______ Kandidaten enden die Shows gut. Sie finden ihren Traumpartner oder ihre Traumpartnerin.	☐	☐

A2 **4 Ergänzen Sie die Reflexivpronomen.**

ich	du	er/es/sie/man	wir	ihr	sie/Sie
freue mich	freust ______	freut ______ ⚠	freuen ______	freut ______	freuen ______ ⚠

5 Schreiben Sie die unterstrichenen Verben richtig.

Fernsehzuschauer können zusehen, wie sich zwei Menschen ~~nenenlerkenn~~ kennenlernen, wie sie sich lieverben,

wie sie sich enfreu oder wie sie sich über den anderen ernärg und sich tenstrei.

6 Ergänzen Sie die richtige Form von *ärgern* oder *freuen* und die Reflexivpronomen.

a Jonas ärgert ______, wenn er schon wieder am Wochenende arbeiten muss.
b Ihr ______ ______ sicher, wenn euer Urlaub jetzt endlich beginnt.
c Ich ______ ______ immer, wenn mein Lieblingslied im Radio gespielt wird.
d Frau Neuhold ______ ______, wenn sie lange auf den Bus warten muss.
e ______ du ______ auch, wenn dein E-Mailprogramm auf dem Computer nicht funktioniert?
f Wir ______ ______, wenn wir am Wochenende bei schönem Wetter wandern können.
g Konrad und Liam ______ ______, wenn sie beim Tennis verlieren.
h Sie ______ ______ sicher, wenn Sie Ihre Tochter wiedersehen, Herr Steiner.

7 Ordnen Sie die Verben zu und schreiben Sie die Imperative mit Reflexivpronomen.

sich konzentrieren · sich umziehen · sich anmelden · sich streiten · sich entspannen · ~~sich vorbereiten~~

a ● Nächste Woche habe ich meine Führerscheinprüfung.
■ Dann bereite dich gut vor, die Prüfung ist nicht so einfach.
b ● Wir möchten auch gern den Deutschkurs besuchen.
■ Dann ________ euch schnell ________, es sind nur noch wenige Plätze frei.
c ● Ich schaffe diese Grammatikübung nicht.
■ ________ ________, dann schaffst du sie sicher.
d ● Ich muss unbedingt meine E-Mails lesen, vielleicht gibt es in der Firma ein Problem.
■ ________ ________ doch, im Urlaub soll man keine E-Mails lesen.
e ● Christoph glaubt, er hat immer recht, aber ich sage ihm trotzdem meine Meinung.
■ ________ ________ nicht, ihr findet sicher eine Lösung.
f ● Ich bin im Regen Rad gefahren.
■ Dann ________ ________ schnell ________, sonst liegst du morgen krank im Bett.

8 Was passt? Ordnen Sie zu.

1 2 3 4 5 6

a [2] Herr Trummer wäscht sein Auto.
b [ ] Kevin ärgert sich.
c [ ] Frau Schulz zieht ihren Sohn an.
d [ ] Kevin ärgert den Hund.
e [ ] Herr Trummer wäscht sich.
f [ ] Frau Schulz zieht sich an.

Tipp Grammatik
Einige Verben müssen immer ein Reflexivpronomen bekommen, z. B. *sich konzentrieren.*
Andere Verben können ein Reflexivpronomen bekommen, z. B. *sich waschen*. Ergänzen Sie diese Information in ihrer Wortschatzliste, z. B. so: *konzentrieren (sich), waschen (auch: sich)* …

▶ 150–153 **9 Was machen die Personen?**
Hören Sie und kreuzen Sie die richtigen Sätze an.

a [ ] Monika duscht sich. [ ] Monika duscht ihre Tochter.
b [ ] Günter zieht sich an. [ ] Karin zieht Günter an.
c [ ] Mia wäscht sich. [ ] Mia wäscht die Wäsche.
d [ ] Dennis ärgert sich. [ ] Der Angestellte ärgert Dennis.

A3 **10 Alltag: Andreas und Julia am Sonntag. Ergänzen Sie die Verben und die Reflexivpronomen.**
Was meinen Sie, was ist Julia von Beruf?

entspannen · anziehen · vorbereiten · ~~duschen~~ · bewegen · treffen · fühlen

Julia: „Ich stehe am Sonntag um acht Uhr auf, dann dusche ich mich (a) und mache das Frühstück. Andreas schläft meistens bis neun. Nach dem Frühstück ________ wir ________ ________ (b). Andreas zieht gleich seine Tennissachen an. Er spielt jeden Sonntag mit Peter Tennis. Er muss ________ ________ (c), sagt er, auch am Sonntag. Wir ________ ________ (d) dann wieder zum Mittagessen. Nach dem Essen ________ wir ________ (e). Andreas ________ ________ (f) dann manchmal müde und schläft eine Viertelstunde. Am Nachmittag gehen wir manchmal in die Stadt oder ins Kino. Am Abend muss ich meistens Hefte korrigieren und ________ ________ (g), denn am Montag habe ich wieder Unterricht."

Julia ist … von Beruf.

11 Schreiben Sie fünf Sätze über Ihren Alltag.

Am Morgen stehe ich …
Danach dusche ich mich und ziehe mich an. Dann …
Um … Uhr … / Am Vormittag / Am Nachmittag /
Am Abend treffe ich mich mit … / …

B

B1 **1** **Auf dem Amt. Schreiben Sie die Wörter richtig und ordnen Sie die Bilder zu.**

1 2 3 4 5 6 7 8 9

a [3] eine BÜHRGE ______ bezahlen
b [ ] einen MPSTEEL ______ bekommen
c [ ] der AMTEBE ______ hat Informationen
d [ ] ein MUFORLAR ______ ausfüllen
e [ ] einen Umzug LDMEEN ______
f [ ] die REPAPIE ______ abgeben
g [ ] ein Formular SCHREITERUNBEN ______
h [ ] der Reisepass ist GABELFENAU ______
i [ ] am TERSCHAL ______ warten

▶ 154 **2** **Was wissen Sie noch? Hören Sie noch einmal. Sind die Sätze richtig oder falsch? Korrigieren Sie die falschen Sätze.**

		richtig	falsch	
a	Die Frau ist auf dem Amt, weil ~~sie ihren Führerschein abholen möchte.~~	[ ]	X	ihr Pass abgelaufen ist
b	Die Frau muss am Automaten eine Nummer ziehen und warten.	[ ]	[ ]	
c	Die Frau braucht ein blaues Formular und zwei Passfotos.	[ ]	[ ]	
d	Die Frau findet, dass sie auf ihren Passfotos gut aussieht.	[ ]	[ ]	
e	Die Frau zeigt Fotos von ihrer Schwester und ihrem Bruder.	[ ]	[ ]	
f	Sie findet, dass ihr Bruder so wie sie aussieht.	[ ]	[ ]	
g	Die Frau möchte noch andere Fotos zeigen.	[ ]	[ ]	

▶ 154 **3** **Hören Sie noch einmal und ergänzen Sie die richtigen Adjektive.**

a Ich brauche **einen** neu**en** Reisepass, **der** ______**e** Pass ist abgelaufen. …
b Außerdem brauchen Sie zwei ______**e** Passfotos, und Sie müssen **ein** ______**es** Formular ausfüllen.
c Man sieht, dass wir Schwestern sind: **die** ______**en** Haare, **das** ______**e** Gesicht, **die** ______**en** Augen …
d Das ist unser Bruder, **ein** ______**er** Mann. **Die** ______**en** Augen hat er von unserer Mutter und auch **die** ______**e** Nase. **Eine** ______**e** Brille hat er auch, und er trägt ______**e** T-Shirts.

4 **Ergänzen Sie die Endungen und die Beispiele. Ordnen Sie dann die Wörter zu.**

eine gute Figur   gute Freunde   ~~mit einer neuen Brille~~   ein neues Formular   ein runder Stempel
die blauen Augen   das alte Foto   der freundliche Beamte   die hohe Gebühr

Regeln	Beispiele	
Hauptregel (HR): meistens -en	ein en neuen Pass	mit einer neuen Brille, …
Singularregel 1 (SR1): nach • der, • das, • die, eine ____	der alt____ Pass	
Singularregel 2 (SR2): nach ein • ____, • ____	ein grün____ Formular ein attraktiv____ Mann	
Pluralregel 1 (PL1): • „Nullartikel" (ohne Artikel) im Nominativ und Akkusativ ____	alt____ T-Shirts	

5 **Was sagt man wo? Auf dem Amt oder auf dem Bahnhof?**
Ergänzen Sie die Endungen und kreuzen Sie an.

		auf dem Amt	auf dem Bahnhof
a	Wann kommt der nächst e Zug?	[ ]	X
b	Sie müssen für den neu____ Pass das weiß____ Formular ausfüllen.	[ ]	[ ]
c	Wir hätten gern zwei günstig____ Fahrkarten nach Braunschweig.	[ ]	[ ]
d	Wie kann ich einen neu____ Führerschein bekommen?	[ ]	[ ]
e	Kann ich das groß____ Fahrrad auch mitnehmen?	[ ]	[ ]
f	Ich war schon in der letzt____ Woche hier. Ist mein Pass heute fertig?	[ ]	[ ]
g	Ich bin Friseurin. Gibt es eine frei____ Stelle für mich?	[ ]	[ ]

B2 **6** **Ergänzen Sie die Wörter und die Endungen.**

Hotel Amade Schokoladenkuchen ~~nach Berlin~~ Apfelsaft Käsesorte ~~Rinderbraten~~

a ● Ich fahre morgen _nach Berlin_.
■ Nimmst du den früh___ oder den spät___ Zug?

b ● Ich hätte gern den _Rinderbraten_.
■ Hätten Sie gern eine groß___ oder eine klein___ Portion?

c ● Wir waren im ______ in Salzburg.
■ Hattet ihr ein teur___ oder ein billig___ Zimmer?

d ● Ich hätte gern einen ______.
■ Ein groß___ oder ein klein___ Glas?

e ● Haben Sie ______?
■ Ja, möchten Sie ein groß___ oder ein klein___ Stück?

f ● Was für eine ______ sollen wir kaufen?
■ Ein weich___ Käse passt gut zum Wein, wir brauchen aber auch ein Stück Hartkäse für die Nudeln.

7 **Ergänzen Sie die Endungen und notieren Sie dann, wo Sie was bekommen.**

a **Das** neu_e_ Passbild können Sie im zweiten Stock machen lassen.
b **Den** neu___ Pass bekommen Sie in einer Woche in Zimmer 412 im vierten Stock.
c **Die** richtig___ Unterschrift bekommen Sie im dritten Stock.
d **Die** richtig___ Formulare finden Sie im Internet.
e **Den** rund___ Stempel bekommen Sie im Keller in Zimmer 9.
f **Die** nötig___ Papiere können Sie im ersten Stock in Zimmer 122 abgeben.

Das brauchen Sie für Ihren Reisepass:

	Formulare	→ Passbild	→ Papiere	→ Stempel	→ Unterschrift	→ Pass
Wo?	_im Internet_	___	___	___	___	___

8 **Was gibt es an diesen Orten? Was gibt es dort nicht? Wählen Sie drei Situationen (a–e) und schreiben Sie Sätze wie im Beispiel.**

a auf dem Amt: (groß) Schreibtische – (schnell) Züge – (rund und eckig) Stempel (Pl.) – (fleißig) Beamte (Pl.)
b am Flughafen: (groß) Flugzeuge – (schwer) Koffer (Pl.) – (braun) Kühe – (freundlich) Stewardessen
c im Restaurant: (interessant) Speisekarten – (hoch) Berge – (klein) Gabeln und Löffel – (sympathisch) Kellnerinnen
d im Supermarkt: (voll) Regale – (reif) Bananen – (groß) Töpfe – (saftig) Schinken (Sg.) – (laut) Motoren
e im Park: (weich) Betten – (klein) Kinder – (interessant) Spielplätze – (gemütlich) Bänke – (schön) Blumen

a Auf dem Amt gibt es große Schreibtische, runde und eckige Stempel und fleißige Beamte. Schnelle Züge gibt es dort nicht.

9 **Lesen Sie die Anzeigen und ergänzen Sie die Endungen. Ordnen Sie dann die Fotos und Firmennamen zu.**

a ☐ Wollen Sie ein wunderschön_es_ Familienfoto machen lassen? Feiern Sie ein groß___ Fest? Oder brauchen Sie nur ein Foto für den neu___ Reisepass? Wir sind genau die richtig___ Adresse für Sie. Vom schnell___ Passbild bis zum groß___ Poster bekommen Sie bei uns alles, was Sie wünschen.
Wir sind umgezogen: Das neu___, groß___ Fotostudio liegt in der Sackstraße 12, im wunderschön___ Stadtzentrum von Graz. Besuchen Sie uns doch.

b ☐ Freuen Sie sich auf den neu___ Führerschein! Unangenehm___ Prüfungsängste können Sie vergessen. Die freundlich___ Fahrlehrer und Fahrlehrerinnen in unseren Kursen bereiten Sie perfekt auf die nötig___ Prüfungen vor, und bald können Sie mit dem eigen___ Auto zum täglich___ Arbeitsplatz oder in den Urlaub fahren.
Die nächst___ Kurs- und Prüfungstermine finden Sie auf unserer Internetseite: www.fahrschulerix.de.

1 Klick – Ihr Fotostudio

2 Lern mit uns, fahr mit uns – Fahrschule Rix

C

C1 **1 Was wissen Sie noch? Lesen Sie noch einmal** → KB S. 122, C1b **und kreuzen Sie an.**

a Eine Umfrage hat gezeigt, dass
- ☐ die beste Freundin sehr wichtig ist.
- ☐ viele Frauen ohne ihren Ehepartner leben wollen.
- ☐ von 1000 Frauen 92 Prozent keinen Partner wollen.

b Wenn die beste Freundin eine Familie hat,
- ☐ bleibt weniger Zeit für die Beziehung.
- ☐ werden Telefongespräche wichtiger.
- ☐ trifft man sich öfter im Café.

c Männerfreundschaften
- ☐ halten nicht länger als zehn Jahre.
- ☐ sind anders als Freundschaften zwischen Frauen.
- ☐ finden die Psychologen weniger interessant.

d Frauen
- ☐ sprechen gern über Erfahrungen.
- ☐ tauschen ihre Gesprächspartnerinnen aus.
- ☐ sprechen nicht gern über ihre Gefühle.

e Männer
- ☐ sind gern gemeinsam aktiv.
- ☐ sehen gern Sportsendungen.
- ☐ verbringen viel Zeit allein mit ihren Hobbys.

Tipp Lesen
Bei Prüfungen bekommen Sie oft Texte mit Mehrfachwahlaufgaben (Multiple Choice). Die Aufgabe gibt Ihnen wichtige Informationen über den Text. Markieren Sie, was vielleicht richtig oder falsch ist. Lesen Sie dann den Text und suchen Sie die Lösungen.

C2 **2 Ergänzen Sie die Formen von *dürfen* und *lassen*.**

dürfen	lassen
a Ich _darf_ in Monikas Wohnung wohnen.	h Ich ______ Monika in meiner Wohnung wohnen.
b Du ______ in Monikas Wohnung wohnen.	i Du ______ Monika in deiner Wohnung wohnen.
c Erich ______ in Monikas Wohnung wohnen.	j Erich _lässt_ Monika in seiner Wohnung wohnen.
d Wir ______ in Monikas Wohnung wohnen.	k Wir ______ Monika in unserer Wohnung wohnen.
e Ihr ______ in Monikas Wohnung wohnen.	l Ihr ______ Monika in eurer Wohnung wohnen.
f Sabine und Kurt ______ in Monikas Wohnung wohnen.	m Sabine und Kurt ______ Monika in ihrer Wohnung wohnen.
g ______ Sie in Monikas Wohnung wohnen, Frau Kern?	

3 Was passt am besten? Ergänzen Sie.

Die Polizei ~~Mein Freund~~ Der Beamte Unser Hund Meine Freundin Unser Chef

a _Mein Freund_ lässt mich sein neues Motorrad ausprobieren.
b ______ lässt uns in ihrer Wohnung wohnen.
c ______ lässt uns am Schalter warten.
d ______ lässt euch nicht weiterfahren.
e ______ lässt uns im August keinen Urlaub nehmen.
f ______ lässt Tims Katze nicht in unseren Garten.

4 Ergänzen Sie die richtigen Formen von *dürfen* oder *lassen*.

a In der Bibliothek _darf_ man sich nicht laut unterhalten.
b Der Kursleiter ______ uns alle Grammatikübungen zu Hause machen.
c ______ ihr im Büro rauchen?
d ______ du mich mit deinem Fahrrad fahren?
e Wir ______ im Park nicht Fußball spielen.
f In Deutschland ______ Jugendliche ab 18 wählen.

5 Ergänzen Sie die Wünsche.

ein Moped haben | ein Tattoo haben | mit den anderen Hunden spielen | Fußball spielen | ~~am Sonntag später aufstehen~~ | am Meer sein

a Frau Bäcker *würde gern am Sonntag später aufstehen*, aber ihre Katze lässt sie nicht schlafen.
b Renate ______, aber ihre Eltern lassen sie kein Moped kaufen.
c Peter ______, aber seine Mitschüler lassen ihn nicht mitspielen.
d Marianne ______, aber ihre Chefin lässt sie keinen Urlaub nehmen.
e Julian ______, aber seine Eltern lassen ihn nicht zum Tattoostudio gehen.
f Mein Hund ______, aber ich lasse ihn nicht frei laufen.

C3 **6** Kennenlernen im Sprachtandem. Was passt? Schreiben Sie die Themen zu den Redemitteln und sammeln Sie weitere Redemittel.

Gefühle | Heimatstadt | Ausbildung und Beruf | Einkaufen | Hobbys | ~~Familie~~ | Tagesablauf | Wetter

a *Familie* — *Ich habe ... Geschwister. Mein/Meine ... heißt und ist ... alt. Ich habe auch ... Haustier(e).*
b ______ — *Ich wohne in ... | Die Stadt ist/hat ... | Es gibt ... | Meine Wohnung ...*
c ______ — *In meiner Freizeit ... ich gern ... | Am liebsten ... | Ich mag/finde ... | Mir gefällt ... Im Urlaub ...*
d ______ — *Ich bin manchmal/oft/immer ... müde/fröhlich ... | Ich ärgere/freue mich, wenn ...*
e ______ — *Ich stehe jeden Tag ... um ... auf. Dann ...*
f ______ — *Ich mag keinen Regen/... | Ich finde es gut, wenn ... | Im Sommer ... ich gern ...*
g ______ — *Ich bin ... von Beruf. | Ich habe ... abgeschlossen.*
h ______ — *Ich kaufe gern/... ein. | Ich trage gern ... | Am liebsten kaufe ich ...*

a Meine/Mein ... heißt ... Sie/Er ist ... von Beruf ...

7 Schreiben Sie kurze persönliche Texte zu zwei Themen aus 6.

Aussprache

1 Ergänzen Sie die Endungen. Welche zwei Themen passen am besten? Ordnen Sie zu.

Familie | Einkaufen | Tagesablauf | Wetter | Ausbildung und Beruf

a ______

ein sym|pa|thi|sch*er* Leh|rer
ein ge|müt|li|ch___ Bü|ro
die al|t___ Schu|le
ei|ne an|stren|gen|d___ Ar|beit
in|tel|li|gen|t___ Schü|ler
ein star|k___ Kaf|fee mit ei|nem klei|n___ Stück Zu|cker
ei|ne in|te|res|san|t___ Fir|ma mit in|ter|na|tio|na|l___ Ge|schäfts|ver|bin|dun|gen

b ______

ein mo|der|n___ Ge|schäft
ein be|son|de|r___ An|ge|bot
fri|sch___ Äp|fel
ein freund|li|ch___ Ver|käu|fer
ein ho|h___ Preis
die prak|ti|sch___ Kre|dit|kar|te
ein lang|___ Re|gal mit vie|len ver|schie|de|n___ Wurst|sor|ten
der neu|___ Su|per|markt im na|h___ Ein|kaufs|zen|trum

▶ 155–156 **2** Hören Sie und sprechen Sie nach. Achten Sie genau auf die Betonung und den Rhythmus.

Tipp Aussprache
Es ist wichtig, dass Sie deutsche Wörter richtig betonen. Wenn Sie lange und schwierige Wörter lernen, sollten Sie immer auch den Wortakzent markieren, z. B. so: Geschäftsverbindung.

Schreibwerkstatt

1 Lesen Sie die Texte. Welches Foto passt zu welchem Text?

Die besten Kennenlerngeschichten …

A ☐ Es war auf einem Familienfest. Nazim, ein Freund meines Vaters hatte ein Foto dabei. Auf dem Foto war ein junger Mann. „Das ist mein Sohn Kenan, er studiert in Ankara", erzählte er. Auf dem Foto war ein netter junger Mann. Er hatte ein ovales Gesicht, braune Augen, kurze schwarze Haare und einen Bart. Außerdem war da eine Handynummer. „Vielleicht solltet ihr euch einmal kennenlernen", hat mein Vater gemeint, und auch meine Mutter war dafür. Das Foto hat mir gefallen, und ich habe Kenan angerufen. Er hat damals in der Türkei gelebt, ich in Deutschland. Auch er hatte inzwischen ein Foto von mir. Wir haben ein paar Mal telefoniert. Aber am Telefon sind wir uns fremd geblieben. Mein Vater hat mir dann ein Flugticket gegeben, und ich bin in die Türkei geflogen. Ich habe Kenan getroffen, habe mich verliebt, und wir haben geheiratet. Kenan ist dann nach Deutschland gezogen. Das Leben hier gefällt ihm und wir machen viel gemeinsam: Wir kochen, wir wandern, wir sehen fern … Aber das Wichtigste ist: Wir verstehen uns.

Sema Kavuk

1

B ☐ Ich habe Miriam bei der Arbeit getroffen. Ich bin Sportjournalistin, und Miriam hat damals bei einer Zeitung als Fotografin gearbeitet. Wir waren beide bei einem Basketballspiel. Es war kurz vor Spielende und auf dem Spielfeld war wirklich viel los. Doch plötzlich konnte ich nichts mehr sehen. Eine große, blonde Frau hat direkt vor mir gestanden und hat fotografiert. Ich konnte die wichtigsten Szenen im Spiel also nicht sehen und habe mich sehr geärgert. Ich habe laut geschimpft. Miriam hat mich angesehen und gelacht. Da habe ich meinen Ärger dann vergessen. Nach dem Spiel haben wir zusammen etwas getrunken. Heute treffen wir uns jeden Dienstag und Donnerstag in einem Café und am Wochenende gehen wir manchmal gemeinsam laufen. Miriam ist heute meine beste Freundin. Ich kann ihr alles erzählen.

Marianne Hahn

2

2 Lesen Sie die Texte noch einmal und ergänzen Sie.

	Sema und Kenan	Miriam und Marianne
a Wo und wie haben sich die Personen kennengelernt?	Foto, …	
b Wie sieht der Ehemann / die Freundin aus?		
c Was machen die Personen gemeinsam?		

3 Denken Sie an Verwandte, Bekannte, Kollegen oder Freunde. Wie haben Sie sich kennengelernt? Wie sieht die Person aus? Was machen Sie gemeinsam? Sammeln Sie Ideen und schreiben Sie eine Kennenlerngeschichte.

… ist eine Bekannte / ein Bekannter / …
Ich habe … in … / bei … kennengelernt.
Sie/Er ist … groß / … alt.
Sie/Er hat … Haare, ein … Gesicht, …
Sie/Er trägt gern …
Sie/Er freut/ärgert sich, wenn …
Wir … oft/manchmal …

Mein Freund José
Aussehen: dunkle Haare, braune Augen, schlank, sportlich
Kennenlernen: Fußballspielen im Park
gemeinsame Aktivitäten: Fußball, Basketball

→ Hier können Sie weiterlernen: www.hueber.de/motive

Ist das der Strand, der dir so gefällt?

Lernwortschatz

Einstiegsseite

der Camping-urlaub, -e
das Inland
die Kindheit

A1

die Bergwanderung, -en
die Besichtigung, -en
die Kurzreise, -n
das Mehrbettzimmer, -
die Ordnung
der/das Prospekt, -e
der Reiseführer, -
der/das Reiseprospekt, -e
der Rückflug, -¨e
der Sand
der Sandstrand, -¨e
das Tauchen
der Tauchurlaub, -e
die Übernachtung, -en
die Unterkunft, -¨e
der Urlauber, -
die Urlaubsreise, -n

erwarten
tauchen
umsteigen
wegfahren
wohlfühlen (sich)
zurechtkommen

fantastisch
kulturell
perfekt

danach
inklusive
plus
vorgestern
ziemlich

A2

der Nachbar, -n
die Reinigung, -en
der Pool, -s
die Zahnbürste, -n

bezahlt
furchtbar
gültig

abends
dienstags
donnerstags
freitags
mittags
mittwochs
montags
morgens
nachmittags
samstags
sonntags
vormittags
wochentags

B1

das Ausflugsprogramm, -e
die Besonderheit, -en
der Blick, -e
die Dachterrasse, -n
die Fitness
der Fitnessraum, -¨e
der Geschäftsmann, -¨er
die Geschäftsreise, -n
der Internetzugang
die Lage, -n
die Parkmöglichkeit, -en
die Sauna, Saunas/Saunen
der Service, -s
das Stadtzentrum, -zentren
die Tiefgarage, -n
das WLAN
der Zugang, -¨e

bieten

entfernt
gratis
komfortabel

vor allem

B2

das Apartment, -s
auch: das Appartement, -s
die Decke, -n
A: die Tuchent, -en
das Handtuch, -¨er
die Hotelküche, -n
das Hotelzimmer, -
die Tierpension, -en
das Kissen, -
A: der Polster, ¨

mitarbeiten
renovieren

extra
gerade

B3

der Aufzug, -¨e
die Rezeption, -en
CH *auch:* die Réception, -en
die Treppe, -n
A: die Stiege, -n

führen
schauen

drinnen
drüben
gegenüber
A/CH: vis-à-vis
herauf/herauf-
heraus/heraus-
herein/herein-
herunter/herunter-
hinauf/hinauf-
hinaus/hinaus-
hinein/hinein-
hinunter/hinunter-
rauf/rauf-
raus/raus-
rein/rein-
runter/runter-

C1

die Bahnlinie, -n
die Breite
die Geschwindigkeit, -en
das Gramm, - (g)
A: 10 Gramm = das Dekagramm, -
die Höchstgeschwindigkeit, -en
der ICE, -s
das Kilogramm, - (kg)
der Kilometer, -
die Länge, -n
der Langstreckenflug, -¨e
der Millimeter, -
der Passagier, -e
das Passagierflugzeug, -e
die Sekunde, -n (s)
der Sitzplatz, -¨e
die Strecke, -n
der Stundenkilometer, -

gehören zu

doppelt
schwer
weltweit

Kilometer pro Stunde (km/h)

C2

die Art, -en
der Aufenthalt, -e
die Bezahlung, -en
die Geldbörse, -n
CH: das Portemonnaie, -s
A: die Geldtasche, -n
die Öffnungszeit, -en
der Reifen, -
CH: der Pneu, -s
die Reisetasche, -n
das Umsteigen
die Verspätung, -en

bitten
lösen

runter

A1 **1** Was wissen Sie noch? Lesen Sie noch einmal → KB S. 126, A1c und ergänzen Sie.

a die drei Wochen gedauert hat b der ihn jetzt erwartet c die er jetzt beantworten muss
d der direkt vor ihrem Hotel lag e das auf ihn wartet f die sie auf ihrer Urlaubsreise gemacht haben
g die sie besichtigt haben h ~~der 22 Stunden gedauert hat~~ i die sie beim Tauchen gesehen hat
j die nach Norwegen gehen soll k der immer perfekt vorbereitet war

A Kathrins Rückflug, _h_, war sehr anstrengend. Deshalb ist sie danach auch sehr müde. Aber sie hat viele schöne Fotos von dem weißen Sandstrand, ___. Und sie denkt oft an die vielen Fische, ___. Die waren fantastisch.

B Gerti und Helmut zeigen ihren Freunden Fotos, ___. Sie haben Fotos von allen Sehenswürdigkeiten, ___. Und sie erzählen von ihrem Reiseführer, ___. Gerti und Helmut wollen bald wieder wegfahren. Sie wollen nächstes Jahr eine Kurzreise machen, ___.

C Die Wanderung über die Alpen, ___, war eine wunderbare Erfahrung für Niklas. Er denkt nicht gern an sein Büro, ___. Auch an die vielen E-Mails, ___, will er nicht denken. Der Alltag, ___, wird sicher schwierig.

2 Was ist was? Unterstreichen Sie das richtige Relativpronomen und ordnen Sie dann zu.

a	7	Gepäcksstücke, der/das/<u>die</u> oft groß und schwer sind	1 Flugzeug
b	☐	ein Dokument, der/das/die man am Flughafen oder an der Grenze braucht	2 Reisepass
c	☐	Autos, der/das/die Fluggäste vom Flughafen zum Hotel bringen	3 Zelt
d	☐	eine Übernachtungsmöglichkeit, der/das/die nicht viel kostet	4 Prospekt
e	☐	ein Heft, der/das/die Urlaubsangebote zeigt	5 Taxis
f	☐	ein Verkehrsmittel, der/das/die Touristen schnell nach New York bringen kann	6 Unterkunft
g	☐	ein Platz, der/das/die zum Übernachten da ist	7 ~~Koffer~~

3 Was nervt im Urlaub? Ergänzen Sie.

Koffer, die eine Eintrittskarte, die ein Pool, der ~~ein Hotel, das~~ Nachbarn, die ein Reiseführer, der
eine Zahnbürste, die Regen, der eine Taxifahrt, die ein Hotelzimmer, das Toiletten, die ein Strand, der

a	ein Hotel, das	weit weg vom Strand liegt	g	___	keinen Balkon hat
b	___	kein Wasser hat	h	___	zu schnell spricht
c	___	schmutzig sind	i	___	keine Sonnenschirme hat
d	___	zu Hause im Badezimmer liegt	j	___	jede Nacht furchtbar laut feiern
e	___	eine ganze Woche dauert	k	___	nicht angekommen sind
f	___	nicht mehr gültig ist	l	___	viel zu teuer ist

▶ 157 **4** Vor der Reise. Hören Sie und notieren Sie, wo die Dinge vorher waren und wo sie jetzt sind.

	vorher	jetzt
a • Buch	auf dem Esstisch	in der Reisetasche
b • Hemden		
c • Sonnenhut		
d • Sonnenmilch		
e • Tickets		
f • Reisepass		

• Reisetasche

• Handgepäck

• Koffer

5 Schreiben Sie Relativsätze zu den Dingen in 4.

a Das Buch, das auf dem Esstisch war, ist jetzt …

6 Der Traumurlaub. Lesen Sie die Sätze (1–5 und a–e). Welche Information passt? Ordnen Sie zu und ergänzen Sie.

1 Die Wanderer sitzen vor der Hütte und unterhalten sich.
2 Die Chefin steht vor meinem Schreibtisch und holt mich aus meinem Urlaubstraum.
3 Der Bergsee ist ziemlich kalt.
~~4~~ Die Hütte liegt hoch oben in den Bergen.
5 Der Hund liegt faul vor der Hütte in der Sonne.

a 4 Ich träume von einer kleinen Berghütte, die hoch oben in den Bergen ______.
b ☐ Ich sehe Wanderer, ______ vor der Hütte ______ und sich ______.
c ☐ Ich sehe einen Hund, ______ faul vor der Hütte in der Sonne ______.
d ☐ Ich stehe vor einem wunderschönen Bergsee, ______ aber ziemlich kalt ______.
e ☐ Wer fragt mich da, ob ich die Post schon geholt habe? Ach ja, meine Chefin, ______ vor meinem Schreibtisch ______ und mich aus meinem Urlaubstraum ______.

7 Reisebilder. Was ist das? Finden Sie Erklärungen für die Zeichnungen und schreiben Sie Relativsätze.

1 Namibia | 2 Brasilien | 3 Thailand | 4 USA | 5 Australien | 6 Frankreich

in einer Tüte stecken   man nur von der Seite sehen   ~~um die Ecke gehen~~
an einem Baum sitzen   einkaufen gehen   an einer Orange riechen

a Bild eins ist ein Zebra, das um die Ecke geht.
b Auf Bild zwei ist ein Affe, ______.
c Bild drei zeigt vier Elefanten, ______.
d Auf Bild vier ist eine Briefmarke, ______.
e Auf Bild fünf sieht man ein Känguruh, das ... ______.
f Bild sechs zeigt ein Weißbrot, ______.

A2 **8 Ansichtskarten. Ergänzen Sie Relativsätze. Wer ist mit seinem Urlaub zufrieden ☺, wer nicht ☹? Ergänzen Sie.**

Das Zimmer liegt im ersten Stock.
Die Band spielt jeden Tag im Hotel.
~~Das Hotel seht ihr auf der Karte.~~
Das Wetter war bis jetzt sehr gut für Wanderungen.
Die Bergwanderungen führen zu gemütlichen Berghütten.
Das Urlaubsdorf liegt in den Tiroler Bergen.

A ○

Hallo Ihr Lieben,

wir wohnen jetzt schon drei Tage in dem Hotel, das Ihr auf der Karte seht (a). Unser Zimmer, ______ (b), ist leider ziemlich klein. Auch das Essen ist nicht mehr so gut wie im letzten Jahr. Außerdem nervt die Band, ______ (c). Nächstes Jahr mieten wir uns ein Haus am Strand.

Herzliche Urlaubsgrüße von
Norbert und Emelda

B ○

Lieber Edwin,

Brandeck ist ein kleines Urlaubsdorf, ______ (d). Wir machen jeden Tag Bergwanderungen, ______ (e). Manchmal übernachten wir auch in einer Hütte. Das Wetter, ______ (f), wird am Wochenende schlechter. Aber da sind wir schon wieder zu Hause. Wir freuen uns auf Euch!

Walter und Andrea

9 Ergänzen Sie die Zeitangaben.

vormittags   wochentags   mittags   donnerstags   ~~nachts~~   morgens

a Otto muss zum Arzt gehen, weil er nachts sehr schlecht schläft.
b Im Urlaub gehen wir ______ immer an den Strand, nachmittags machen wir Ausflüge.
c ______ duscht Kevin, dann frühstückt er.
d Dienstags und ______ sind die Kinder nach der Schule bei meiner Mutter.
e Am Sonntag kannst du deine Kleider nicht in die Reinigung bringen. Sie ist nur ______ geöffnet.
f Das Wetter ist typisch für den November. Morgens ist es neblig, ______ sieht man dann manchmal ein bisschen Sonne.

Tipp Wortschatz
abends, mittwochs, wochentags, ...
= jeden Abend, Mittwoch, Wochentag ...

B

B1 **1 Was wissen Sie noch? Lesen Sie noch einmal → KB S. 128, B1a. Welche Unterkunft bietet was? Ergänzen Sie und ordnen Sie zu.**

a gratis Intern _ zu _ ang
b F _ tn _ ss _ aum
c M _ hr _ ettz _ mm _ _
d T _ _ fg _ _ age
e S _ _ na
f _ acht _ rr _ sse
g Bl _ ck auf das St _ dt _ en _ _ um
h Au _ fl _ gs _ _ ogr _ mme

Hotel Lindenhof: a, ... Jugendherberge „Am Park“: ______

B2 **2 Was wissen Sie noch? Hören Sie noch einmal und kreuzen Sie an.**

▶ 158

a Clarissa glaubt,
- ☐ dass sie im Internet ein günstiges Hotel gefunden hat.
- ☐ keine günstigen Hotels finden kann.
- ☐ ein billiges Appartement findet.

b Ein Doppelzimmer in Clarissas Hotel kostet
- ☐ 20 Euro pro Person.
- ☐ 20 Euro für zwei Personen.
- ☐ 20 Euro für zwei Nächte.

c Leandro will wissen,
- ☐ ob das Zimmer einen Balkon hat.
- ☐ ein Bad hat.
- ☐ einen Fernseher hat.

d Das Hotel liegt nicht
- ☐ weit vom Stadtzentrum entfernt.
- ☐ neben der Autobahn.
- ☐ neben dem Bahnhof.

e Das Hotel hat
- ☐ ruhige Zimmer.
- ☐ eine Tiefgarage, die gratis ist.
- ☐ keine Parkmöglichkeiten.

f Das Frühstück
- ☐ ist inklusive.
- ☐ muss man extra bezahlen.
- ☐ kann man nicht im Hotel bekommen.

g Das Zimmer ist günstig,
- ☐ wenn man morgens und abends im Hotel isst.
- ☐ wenn man 40 Euro extra für das Frühstück bezahlt.
- ☐ wenn man länger bleibt.

h Clarissa und Leandro
- ☐ nehmen das Zimmer.
- ☐ wollen mehr Informationen über das Hotel.
- ☐ suchen ein anderes Hotel.

▶ 159–162 **3 Lesen Sie die Sätze und hören Sie dann. Zu welchem Dialog (1–4) passt welches Problem (a–i)? Ergänzen Sie. Achtung, nicht alle Probleme passen!**

a ☐ Die Rechnung stimmt nicht.
b ☐ Das Zimmer hat keinen Meerblick.
c ☐ Im Zimmer ist es sehr laut.
d ☐ Das Licht im Badezimmer funktioniert nicht.
e ☐ Es gibt keine Decken, Kissen und Handtücher.
f 1 Die Heizung funktioniert nicht.
g ☐ Das Zimmer hat kein Bad.
h ☐ Der Zimmerschlüssel passt nicht.
i ☐ Man kann das Fenster nicht öffnen.

▶ 163 **4 Hören Sie und schreiben Sie das Gespräch. Zu welchem Dialog aus 3 passt das Gespräch?**

Was kann ich für Sie tun? Haben Sie einen Wunsch? Kann ich Ihnen helfen? Die Heizung funktioniert nicht. Das Licht in unserem Badezimmer funktioniert nicht. In unserem Zimmer gibt es ein Problem. 442 Sie können ... Ich möchte mich beschweren. Wir haben ein Problem. Was ist denn nicht in Ordnung? Wir reparieren das sofort. Da müssen wir uns entschuldigen. Das tut mir leid. Welche Zimmernummer haben Sie denn? ~~Guten Abend.~~

Rezeptionist: Guten Abend ... Gast: Ich ...
Das passt zu Dialog ...

5 Schreiben Sie Dialoge zu den Situationen aus 3. Verwenden Sie die Sätze aus 4.

B3 **6 Ergänzen Sie.**

Wo?

a vor _ _
b h _ _ _ _ _ _
c o _ _ _
d u _ _ _ _
e l _ _ _ _ _
f r _ _ _ _ _ _
g dri _ _ _ _
h dr _ _ _ _ _ _

Wohin?

i _ _ _ _ ei _
j _ _ _ _ _ us
k _ _ _ _ au _
l _ _ _ _ un _ _ _

7 Ergänzen Sie die Gegenteile zu den unterstrichenen Wörtern.

a ● Müssen wir hier nach links?
■ Nein, unser Zimmer ist rechts.

b ● Kommst du mit an den Strand?
■ Nein, ______ ist es zu heiß, ich bleibe lieber hier drinnen.

c ● Zur Disco müssen wir hier ______.
■ Bist du sicher? Wenn es nicht stimmt, müssen wir die Treppe wieder hinauf.

d ● Ist das Schwimmbad unten im Keller?
■ Nein, es ist ______ auf der Dachterrasse.

e ● Möchtest du im Bus ______ sitzen?
■ Nein, ich sitze lieber vorne.

f ● Ich möchte auch in den Pool. Warte ich komme ______.
■ Ich gehe aber schon wieder hinaus. Das Wasser ist zu kalt.

8 Wo sind die Personen? Ergänzen Sie Adverbien aus 6 und ordnen Sie die Situationen (1–6) zu.

1 im Zelt auf dem Campingplatz

2 vor dem Kino

3 vor dem Eiffelturm

4 an der Bushaltestelle

5 in der Jugendherberge

6 auf einem Berg

a 5 Hier gibt es Stockbetten! Möchtest du lieber oben oder ______ schlafen?
b ☐ Das ist unser Bus. Steigen wir ______ oder ______ ein?
c ☐ Hier ______ scheint die Sonne, ______ im Tal ist Nebel, das sieht toll aus.
d ☐ ● Sie spielen einen Musikfilm. Komm, gehen wir ______.
■ Na gut, aber wenn der Film mir nicht gefällt, gehe ich gleich wieder ______.
e ☐ ______ regnet es. Hier ______ ist es warm und gemütlich. Es ist nur etwas eng.
f ☐ Ich war noch nie auf dem Turm. Ich möchte unbedingt ______.

9 Ergänzen Sie *hin* oder *her*.

a ● Hallo Irmi. Wir warten an der Rezeption.
■ Ich bin in meinem Zimmer im vierten Stock.
● Sollen wir hin auf kommen oder kommst du ______ unter?

b ● Kurt sitzt sicher schon im Flugzeug.
■ Wo fliegt er denn ______?
● Nach New York.
■ Da war ich noch nie, da möchte ich auch einmal ______.

c ● Kann ich mit dem Chef sprechen?
■ Ja, er ist in seinem Büro, gehen Sie ______ ein.
● Haben Sie fünf Minuten Zeit für mich?
▲ Natürlich, kommen Sie ______ ein.

d ● Wer ist das?
■ Das ist doch der Schauspieler, wie heißt er gleich?
● Egal, gehen wir ______.
■ Klar, er kommt sicher nicht ______, dann gehen wir ______.

Aussprache

▶ 164 **1** Hören Sie. Wo hören Sie /r/? Wo hören Sie kein /r/? Markieren Sie wie im Beispiel.

Reiseführer – Reiseführerin
Nachbar – Nachbarin
drüben – vorgestern
runter – her
Fitnessraum – beschweren
war – waren

2 Wann spricht man /r/? Wann spricht man kein /r/? Kreuzen Sie an.

	/r/	kein /r/
a Das *r* ist am Wortanfang oder am Silbenanfang: *Reise, waren*	☐	☐
b Das *r* ist am Wortende oder am Silbenende: *war, vorgestern*	☐	☐

3 Artikelwörter und Nomen. Wo hören Sie /r/? Wo hören Sie kein /r/? Markieren Sie.

ihr Rückflug
unsere Koffer
ihre Trinkflasche
unser Zimmer
euer Urlaub
in Ihrem Prospekt
eure Garage
jeder Frühstücksraum

▶ 165 **4** Hören Sie, vergleichen Sie und sprechen Sie nach.

C1 **1 Welche Frage passt? Ordnen Sie zu.**

a [4] die Länge
b [ ] die Breite
c [ ] die Höhe
d [ ] die Geschwindigkeit
e [ ] die Temperatur
f [ ] die Zeit
g [ ] das Gewicht

1 Wie breit ...? 2 Wie schwer ...?
3 Wie kalt/warm ...? 4 ~~Wie lang ...?~~
5 Wann ...?/ Wie lange ...? / Wie spät ...?
6 Wie hoch ...? 7 Wie schnell ...?

2 Schreiben Sie die Wörter mit Plural und ordnen Sie die Abkürzungen zu.

mm cm m km km/h h ' (min) " (s) ° t ~~g~~ kg

a ~~das GMRMA~~
b der ERMET
c der MEKILOTER
d die MITENU
e der KILODENSTUNMETER
f der TERLIMEMIL
g die DESTUN
h der TIMETERZEN
i die KUNSEDE
j die NETON
k das KIGRAMMLO
l der RAGD

a das Gramm, - (g) b ...

3 Tauschen Sie die markierten Wörter und korrigieren Sie so die Fehler.

Das schnellste Fahrrad und das kleinste Auto

Ist das **eRockit** ein Fahrrad? Die Frage kann man gar nicht so klar beantworten. Man fährt auf dem eRockit wie auf einem Fahrrad, die Arbeit macht aber ein starker E-Motor. Für ein Fahrrad ist das eRockit auch ziemlich schwer. Es wiegt ~~ein Meter dreißig~~ 123 Kilogramm. Es kann aber bis zu 60 Kilogramm schnell fahren, und das ist viel schneller als ein normales Fahrrad. Einen Parkplatz muss man natürlich auch nicht suchen. Das Fahrrad ist nur 45 Stundenkilometer lang.

Auch mit dem **Peel** ist die Parkplatzsuche kein Problem. Der Peel ist das kleinste Auto der Welt und sogar noch ein bisschen kleiner als das eRockit. Er ist nur ~~123 Kilogramm~~ ein Meter dreißig lang, und ein Meter zwanzig hoch. Er fährt nur ein Meter vierzig, und das mit einem E-Motor. Das Auto ist auch viel leichter als das eRockit. Es wiegt 81 Stundenkilometer.

4 Ergänzen Sie die Adjektive im Superlativ.

schwierig günstig ~~schnell~~ groß ~~klein~~ interessant

a Erik, Marko und ich haben alle Internet. Markos Netz ist am schnellsten.
b Der Peel ist das kleinste Auto.
c Wir sind mit dem Airbus A 380 in die USA geflogen. Er ist ________ Flugzeug.
d Sandro interessiert sich für viele Sportarten, ________ findet er Basketball.
e Wir sollten nicht ________ Hotel nehmen. Für eine schöne Unterkunft bezahle ich gern ein bisschen mehr.
f Ich finde, Finnisch oder Russisch sind keine einfachen Sprachen, aber ________ ist sicher Chinesisch.

> **Tipp Grammatik**
> Wenn der Superlativ zum Verb gehört, müssen Sie *am* + *-sten* benutzen, z. B.: *Er fährt am schnellsten.*
> Wenn der Superlativ vor einem Nomen steht, dürfen Sie kein *am* verwenden, z. B.: *Das eRockit ist das schnellste Fahrrad.*

C2 ▶ 166–168 **5 Hören Sie und beantworten Sie die Fragen.**

Verspätung Leute Sturm/Bauchschmerzen Taxifahrer München Stau/Kälte Ärztin Neapel New Orleans Flugzeug Auto Schiff

a Wohin sind die Personen gefahren?
b Wie sind die Personen gereist?
c Was war das Problem auf der Reise?
d Wer hat geholfen?

Dialog 1: a Nach ...

6 **Beschreiben Sie ein Reiseproblem aus 5. Beschreiben Sie dann ein Problem, das Sie selbst auf einer Reise hatten.**

Ich bin mit ... von ... nach ... geflogen/gefahren/...
... hatte Verspätung ... Ich musste ...
... hat/haben geholfen.

7 **Eine Wandersage (zu „Wandersage" s. auch Kursbuch, Seite 66).**
Lesen Sie den Text und beantworten Sie die Fragen.

Die vergessenen Kinder
Herr und Frau M. fahren mit ihrem Wohnwagen in den Urlaub. Die Kinder der Familie spielen auf der Rückbank des Autos, werden aber bald müde. Weil man im großen Bett des Wohnwagens viel besser als im Auto schlafen kann, lassen Herr und Frau M. ihre Kinder in den Wohnwagen steigen. Nach zwei Stunden bleibt Herr M. auf dem Parkplatz einer Autobahnraststätte mit einem Restaurant stehen. Die Kinder wachen auf, öffnen die Tür des Wohnwagens und laufen auf den Spielplatz des Restaurants. Die Eltern der Kinder kommen bald zurück, sehen die Kinder nicht und fahren weiter. Nach einer Stunde wird Herr M. von der Polizei angehalten. Zwei Polizisten kontrollieren die Papiere des Fahrers und den Wohnwagen. Da wird den Eltern plötzlich klar, dass sie ihre Kinder auf dem Parkplatz der Autobahnraststätte vergessen haben. Doch da sehen sie hinter den Fenstern des Polizeiautos die frohen Gesichter ihrer Kinder. Jetzt müssen Herr und Frau M. nur noch ihr Problem mit der Polizei lösen.

Wohnwagen

a Wo lassen Herr und Frau M. ihre Kinder auf der Reise schlafen?
b Was passiert auf dem Parkplatz des Restaurants an der Autobahn?
c Warum werden Herr und Frau M. von der Polizei angehalten?

Tipp Grammatik
Die Artikelendungen für den Dativ und Genitiv können Sie sich auch rhythmisch merken. Sprechen Sie die Endungen und klopfen Sie den Rhythmus.
Dativ: em/em/er/en + -n -/-/-/..
Genitiv: es+s/es+s/er/er ../../-/-

8 **Lesen Sie den Text in 7 noch einmal. Wo steht der Genitiv? Schreiben Sie die Satzteile mit Genitiv und auch den Nominativ.**

Genitiv	Nominativ
die Kinder der Familie	die Familie

9 **Ergänzen Sie den Genitiv.**

die Tür	• des Wohnwagens	eines Wohnwagens	-es (Nomen + s)
die Rückbank	• des Autos		-es (Nomen + s)
der Parkplatz	• der Autobahnraststätte		-er
die Gesichter	• der Kinder	ihrer Kinder	-er

10 **Was möchten Sie wissen, wenn ...? Ordnen Sie zu. Schreiben Sie dann Fragen wie im Beispiel.**

Abfahrt des Zuges   Zufriedenheit der anderen Gäste   ~~Lage des Hotels~~   Farbe des Autos
Preis der Fahrkarte   Höhe der Wagenmiete   Preis der Zimmer   Größe der Zimmer   Dauer der Reise
Größe des Autos   Höchstgeschwindigkeit des Autos   Ankunft des Zuges

Was möchten Sie wissen, wenn ...
a ... Sie ein Hotelzimmer im Internet suchen?
b ... Sie ein Auto mieten wollen?
c ... eine Zugreise planen?

a die Lage des Hotels – Wo liegt ...? ...

11 **Ordnen Sie zu und ergänzen Sie den Genitiv.**

Der Pass gehört meiner Freundin.   Das Flugzeug fliegt nach Sidney   ~~Der Motor ist in unserem Auto.~~
Die Ansichtskarte haben unsere Freunde geschrieben   Die Zimmer sind im Hotel Miramare.

a Der Motor *unseres Autos* ist kaputt.
b Der Reisepass ______________ ist nicht mehr gültig.
c Die Zimmer ______________ haben alle Meerblick.
d Ich habe die Ansichtskarte ______________ noch nicht gelesen.
e Man hat den Abflug ______________ verschoben.

Schreibwerkstatt

1 Lesen Sie die Texte und ordnen Sie die Fotos aus dem Reiseblog zu.

1 

2 

3 

VON OSTEN NACH WESTEN – ZEHN WOCHEN IN DEN USA

A ☐ 14. 5.: Wir sind gestern sehr spät am Flughafen in New York angekommen. Die Reise war lang und anstrengend, aber es hat alles geklappt. Das Taxi, das uns zum Hotel gebracht hat, war natürlich gelb. Für New Yorker Taxis ein Muss. Von unserem Hotel haben wir einen schönen Blick auf die Stadt. Das Foto, das ihr hier seht, haben wir heute Morgen vom Dach unseres Hotels gemacht. Unser Zimmer ist klein, sauber und nicht sehr teuer. Die Unterkunft ist also o. k. New York, wir kommen ...!

B ☐ 17. 5. Nach dem Abendessen im Chinarestaurant sind wir nicht mehr hungrig. Zu zweit schaffen wir aber doch noch ein bisschen Nachspeise. Das Mädchen, das ihr neben mir seht, ist eine Freundin aus Österreich, die wir in New York getroffen haben. Die Welt ist klein ...

C ☐ 29. 6. Wir sind jetzt schon fast sechs Wochen unterwegs. Wir haben viel gesehen. Besonders die Nationalparks finden wir toll. Der Park, der uns am besten gefällt, ist der Yosemite Nationalpark.
Das Foto zeigt euch einen meiner Lieblingsplätze, es gibt aber noch viele andere ... Heute Abend geht's weiter nach San Francisco. Die nächste Stadt wartet auf uns, das ist toll! Aber auch das Ende unserer Reise kommt näher ☹ ...

2 Lesen Sie noch einmal. Wo finden Sie welche Informationen? Notieren Sie.

~~Ankunft~~ Sehenswürdigkeiten Freunde Verkehrsmittel Unterkunft Essen und Trinken Reisetipps

A: Ankunft, ...

3 Suchen Sie zwei oder drei Reise- oder Urlaubsfotos und schreiben Sie zu den Fotos kurze Texte für einen Reiseblog.

Ich bin / Wir sind nach/von ... nach ... gereist.
Wir haben eine Reise nach/durch ... gemacht.
Wir sind am ... in ... angekommen.
Auf dem Foto seht ihr das Flugzeug / den Bus ..., der/das/die uns zu/nach ... gebracht hat.
Unsere Unterkunft war ...
Wir haben ... gesehen/gegessen/getrunken/getroffen.

→ Hier können Sie weiterlernen: www.hueber.de/motive

Lernwortschatz

Einstiegsseite
die Ausstellung, -en
das E-Book, -s
die Kultur, -en
die Oper, -n
die Rockmusik
das Video, -s

ausleihen
A: ausborgen
malen

Ausstellungen besuchen
in einer Band spielen
ins Museum gehen
Musik machen
Theater spielen

A1
die Aktion, -en
die Beschreibung, -en
der Bürger, -
die Gruppe, -n
das Medium, Medien
die Mitteilung, -en
die Popkultur
die Regierung, -en
die Stadtregierung, -en
die Suche
das Treffen, -
die Veranstaltung, -en
das Versteck, -e

achtgeben
interessieren (sich)
irren (sich)
nennen
pflanzen
unternehmen
verabreden
verstecken

kritisch
still

dabei
nämlich
zusammen/zusammen-

liegen bleiben
vorbei sein

A2
Basketball
der Müll
CH: der Abfall, ¨-e

sich ärgern über
beginnen mit
einladen zu
erzählen von
fragen nach
sich freuen über
sich interessieren für
sich kümmern um
schreiben über
sprechen mit
sprechen über
suchen nach

B1
die Fotografie, -n
der Tanz, ¨-e
der Tanzkurs, -e
das Theaterstück, -e

B2
die Flöte, -n

besorgen
vorhaben

wahrscheinlich

einen Plan haben

B3
das Interesse, -n

reden
reden mit
reden über

B4
der Eintritt
die Eintrittskarte, -n
CH: das Billett, -e
die Frage nach
der Terminvorschlag, ¨-e
die Überstunde, -n

B5
das Orchester, -
der Spielfilm, -e

C1
die Aussprache
die Bewerbung, -en
das Bewerbungsgespräch, -e
Deutsch
die Hochschule, -n
die Übung, -en

lügen
übersetzen
sich konzentrieren auf

auswendig
deutlich
ehrlich

auswendig lernen
seine Grenzen suchen
an die Grenzen gehen

C2
der Alkohol
die Bohne, -n
A: die Fisole, -n (grüne Bohne)
der Briefumschlag, ¨-e
CH: das Couvert, -s
die Creme, -s
das Feuerzeug, -e
das Holz
der Knopf, ¨-e
die Linie, -n
das Loch, ¨-er
die Mülltonne, -n
CH: die Abfalltonne, -n
das Parfüm, -s
der Stoff, -e
das Streichholz, ¨-er
A: die Zünder (Pl.)
die Taste, -n
der Turm, ¨-e
die Tüte, -n
A: das Sackerl, -n
CH: der Sack, ¨-e

verwenden

C3
der Anfang, ¨-e
das Notebook, -s

erinnern (sich)

automatisch
deprimiert
fröhlich
schief

A1 **1** Was wissen Sie noch? Lesen Sie noch einmal → KB S. 134, A1b. Ergänzen Sie die Antworten (1–7) und ordnen Sie sie zu.

pflanzen still Mitteilung achtgegeben ~~irren~~ Verstecken Müll

a 5 Warum sehen Experten das Internet kritisch?
b ☐ Wofür verabredet man sich gern im Internet?
c ☐ Was taten die Teilnehmer an einer Flashmob-Aktion in Braunschweig und Wien?
d ☐ Worüber ärgern sich Stadtregierungen und Bürger nach Outdoor-Clubbing-Partys?
e ☐ Worum kümmern sich Personen, die an Guerilla Gardening-Aktionen teilnehmen?
f ☐ Wonach suchen Geocacher?
g ☐ Wozu hat eine Hamburger Jugendliche in ihrem sozialen Netzwerk eingeladen?

1 Zu ihrer Geburtstagsparty. Sie hat bei ihrer Einladung nicht ____________, und 1600 Personen sind gekommen.
2 Sie standen zehn Minuten ganz ____________ auf einem Platz und sahen in den Nachthimmel.
3 Über den ____________ auf den Straßen und in den Parks.
4 Für Partys, Feste oder Ausflüge. Meist informiert eine kurze ____________ darüber, wo und wann die Veranstaltung stattfindet.
~~5~~ Weil sie glauben, dass das Internet uns keine Zeit für die Familie und Freunde lässt. Aber sie _irren_ sich.
6 Um hässliche Plätze in der Stadt. Dort ____________ sie Blumen und Gemüse.
7 Nach ____________ in der Natur.

A2 **2** Ordnen Sie zu und schreiben Sie die Verben mit Präposition.

a Frau Seidel **ärgert** sich 7
b Herr Stein **erzählt** ☐
c Anita **freut** sich ☐
d Mark **sucht** im Internet ☐
e Wolfgang und Gabriele **laden** ihre Freunde ☐
f Irena **kümmert** sich ☐
g Sophie **denkt** oft ☐
h Der Pianist Pawel Novak **beginnt** sein Konzert ☐

1 **mit** einem Stück von Chopin.
2 **um** das Hochzeitsvideo.
3 **zu** ihrem neuen Theaterstück ein.
4 **von** seinem neuen E-Book.
5 **über** (+ Akk.) die Karten für die Oper.
6 **nach** Flash-Mob-Aktionen.
7 ~~**über** (+ Akk.) die hohen Eintrittspreise für die Kunstausstellung.~~
8 **an** (+ Akk.) die französischen Filme, die sie in Paris gesehen hat.

a sich ärgern über (+ Akk.), b ...

3 Wofür interessieren sich diese Personen aus 2? Was meinen Sie? Ordnen Sie zu und schreiben Sie Sätze wie im Beispiel.

~~Frau Seidel~~ Anita Mark Irena

für die Videokamera von ihrem Freund Leo für Popkultur
~~für die Bilder von Picasso~~ für die CD von Verdis Oper „Aida"

Frau Seidel interessiert sich vielleicht für die Bilder von Picasso.
Anita ...

Tipp Wortschatz und Grammatik
Lernen Sie die Verben mit Präpositionen. Achten Sie auch auf den Kasus (Akkusativ oder Dativ). Eine Liste der wichtigsten Verben finden Sie hier: www.hueber.de/motive

4 Ergänzen Sie die richtigen Verben (____) und Präpositionen (~~~~).

entschuldigt gesprochen gewartet ~~kümmern~~ erzählt

a ● Wir fliegen am Wochenende nach Lissabon.
■ Soll ich mich wieder _um_ euren Hund _kümmern_?
b ● Wie lange hast du ~~~~ den Bus ____________?
■ Sicher eine halbe Stunde.
c ● Hast du gehört, Yvonne hat gekündigt.
■ Ja, sie hat mir ~~~~ ihrem Streit mit dem Chef ____________.
d ● Der Rezeptionist hat uns den falschen Zimmerschlüssel gegeben.
■ Ja, aber er hat sich ~~~~ den Fehler ____________.
e ● Wie geht es Werner nach seinem Unfall letztes Wochenende?
■ Ich weiß nicht, ich habe noch nicht ~~~~ ihm ____________.

5 Schlechte Handyverbindungen. Was hast du gesagt?
Ergänzen Sie die Fragewörter (____) und die Antworten (____).

Über unsere neue Wohnung. Um unsere Blumen. Über das schlechte Essen. Über seinen Unfall. Mit dem Training. Für Musik.

Wir haben uns ...

a ● Ich habe mich mit Gernot verabredet. Wir gehen in ein Konzert, obwohl Gernot sich eigentlich nicht ... interessiert.
■ Wofür interessiert er sich nicht?
● ______

b ● Die Zimmer im Hotel waren o. k. Aber wir haben uns ... geärgert.
■ ______ habt ihr euch geärgert?
● ______

c ● Wir treffen uns um sieben, dann können wir sofort ... beginnen.
■ ______ können wir beginnen?
● ______

d ● Wir haben unsere Nachbarin gefragt, aber sie will sich nicht ... kümmern.
■ ______ will sie sich nicht kümmern?
● ______

e ● Mein Bruder ist jetzt drei Tage im Krankenhaus, aber will noch nicht ... sprechen.
■ ______ will er noch nicht sprechen?
● ______

f ● Wir sind umgezogen. Wie freuen uns wirklich ... .
■ ______ freut ihr euch?
● ______

▶ 169 6 Lesen Sie die beiden Ausschnitte aus einem Dialog und ergänzen Sie. Hören Sie dann und vergleichen Sie.

von ~~wofür~~ worüber daran daran woran woran davon ~~dafür~~ wovon

● Hallo Marie.
■ Hallo Lydia.
● Na, willst du dich endlich dafür entschuldigen? (a)
■ Wofür soll ich mich entschuldigen? (b)
● Du weißt schon wofür. Ich muss jeden Tag ______ denken. (c)
■ ______ musst du denken? (d)
● Das solltest du eigentlich wissen.
...

■ Sag mir doch endlich, ______ du dich geärgert hast. (e)
● Sabine hat allen ______ erzählt. (f)
■ ______ hat sie erzählt? (g)
● Na, ______ dir und Dietmar. (h)
Du warst das ganze Wochenende bei ihm. Hast du gar nicht ______ gedacht? (i)
■ ______? (j)
● Na, Dietmar und ich, wir ...

▶ 169 7 Hören Sie noch einmal und ergänzen Sie dann die Namen.

Lydia Marie Marie-Sophie Dietmar

Marie ist ______s beste Freundin. ______ glaubt, dass ______ das ganze Wochenende bei ______ war. Sabine hat davon erzählt. ______ soll sich dafür entschuldigen, denn ______ liebt ______. ______ erklärt ______, dass ______ bei ______ war. ______ ist ______s Cousine.

A3 8 Ein Interview mit Kasim. Schreiben Sie die Fragen zu Kasims Antworten mit den Verben.

denken an ~~(2x)~~ sich kümmern um (2x) sich interessieren für ~~(2x)~~ sich ärgern über (2x)

a Woran denkst du oft? An meine Familie in Istanbul.
b ______? Für Rockmusik.
c ______? Über schlechtes Wetter.
d ______? Um meine Goldfische.
e Für wen interessierst du dich? Für die Fußballspieler von meinem Lieblingsclub.
f ______ oft? An meine Schwester Leyla.
g ______? Über meinen unfreundlichen Nachbarn.
h ______? Um meinen alten Onkel.

Woran denkst du?

Tipp Grammatik

Bei Dingen:	● **Worüber** ärgerst du dich?	■ **Über** das Fernsehprogramm.	● **Darüber** solltest du dich nicht ärgern.
Bei Personen:	● **Über wen** ärgerst du dich?	■ **Über** meinen Bruder.	● **Über ihn** solltest du dich nicht ärgern.

B

B2 **1 Was wissen Sie noch? Hören Sie noch einmal und ordnen Sie zu.**

▶ 170

a	Daniel **hat vor,**	5	1	mit Anna in die Disco zu gehen.
b	Daniel **hat Lust,**		2	Flöte zu spielen.
c	Daniel kann		3	nicht Flöte spielen.
d	Daniel sagt, dass er **angefangen hat,**		4	in ein klassisches Konzert gehen.
e	Daniel glaubt, Anna möchte		5	Anna anzurufen.
f	Daniel **versucht**		6	Konzertkarten zu besorgen.

2 Unterstreichen Sie in 1 die Infinitive mit *zu*.

3 Ergänzen Sie.

Nachts hat sie ein bisschen Angst · Nächsten Monat fange ich an · Ich habe meiner Mutter versprochen · Aber Erich hat es nicht geschafft · Ich helfe dir · Aber Irene hat keine Lust · ~~Seit zwei Stunden versucht er~~ · Unsere Chefin hat verboten

a Herr Hansen muss unbedingt mit seinem Chef sprechen. Seit zwei Stunden versucht er, ihn anzurufen.
b Ich möchte Klavier spielen können. ______, Klavier zu lernen.
c Renate möchte mit ihrer Freundin Irene einen Actionfilm sehen. ______, ins Kino zu gehen.
d Die Raucher in unserer Firma sind unglücklich. ______, im Büro zu rauchen.
e Ich kann am Sonntag nicht wandern gehen. ______, sie im Krankenhaus zu besuchen.
f Die Koffer sind sehr schwer. ______, sie ins Haus zu tragen.
g Ich habe eine Stunde auf ihn gewartet. ______, zu unserer Verabredung zu kommen.
h Sabrina parkt ihr Auto in einer Tiefgarage. ______, ihr Auto aus der Garage zu holen.

4 *Zu* oder kein *zu*? Wer macht Kunst (M), wer erlebt Kunst (E)? Ordnen Sie zu.

a E Am Wochenende regnet es wahrscheinlich. Herr Sommer hat vor, am Samstag DVDs aus zu leihen.
b ☐ Unsere Großmutter hat vor einem halben Jahr begonnen, Bilder ___ malen.
c ☐ Walter macht wirklich gute Fotos. Er will sich eine neue Kamera ___ kaufen.
d ☐ Carina muss für das Konzert am Mittwoch Flöte ___ üben.
e ☐ Techno mag ich nicht. Ich schaffe es nicht, länger als eine Minute zu___ hören.
f ☐ Mein Hund lässt mich nicht in Ruhe ___ lesen. Er will spazieren ___ gehen.

B3 **5 Was wissen Sie noch? Hören Sie noch einmal und ordnen Sie zu.**

▶ 171

a	Anna **findet es nett,**	4	1	bei Verabredungen Handynummern zu tauschen.
b	Lisa **findet es wichtig,**		2	immer das Richtige zu sagen.
c	Anna würde gern		3	mit Daniel essen gehen.
d	Anna meint, **es ist wichtig**		4	~~mit Daniel zu reden.~~
e	Anna **findet es nicht einfach,**		5	gemeinsame Interessen zu haben.

6 Was passt? Ergänzen Sie.

schwierig, Eintrittskarten zu bekommen · anstrengend, so viele Überstunden zu machen · stressig, drei Termine an einem Tag zu haben · langweilig, da stundenlang zuzusehen · ~~unhöflich, zu spät zu kommen~~

a ● Rosi ist eine halbe Stunde zu spät zu unserer Verabredung gekommen.
  ■ Das finde ich gar nicht gut. Es ist sehr unhöflich, zu spät zu kommen.
b ● Wir möchten heute in die Oper gehen.
  ■ Hoffentlich bekommt ihr noch Karten. Ich habe gehört, es ist ______.
c ● Besuchst du mit Pedro das Schachturnier am Wochenende?
  ■ Nein. Es ist sicher ______.

d ● Es ist schon 20:00 Uhr. Arbeitest du gern so lang?
■ Nein, im Gegenteil. Ich finde es sehr ______.
e ● Dein Terminkalender ist sehr voll.
■ Ja, das stimmt. Es ist ______, aber es geht nicht anders.

7 Was stimmt für Sie? Schreiben Sie vier persönliche Sätze.

~~auf kleine Kinder aufpassen~~ noch eine Fremdsprache lernen für 20 Personen kochen eine ganze Nacht lang tanzen bei einem Marathonlauf mitmachen im Winter in einem Zelt übernachten ein Jahr Urlaub machen fliegen lernen 100 Jahre alt werden noch einmal 13 Jahre alt sein in den Weltraum fliegen ...

☺ Es ist toll/interessant/wunderbar/schön/prima/super/...
☹ Es ist schwierig/langweilig/anstrengend/schrecklich/...

☹ Es ist nicht immer einfach, auf kleine Kinder aufzupassen. ☺ Es ist ...

8 Lesen Sie die Tabelle. Suchen Sie in 1–7 Beispielsätze und ordnen Sie sie zu.

bestimmte Verben } Infinitiv mit „zu"	„haben" + Nomen } Infinitiv mit „zu"	„es" + Adjektiv } Infinitiv mit „zu"
Daniel hat vor, ...	Daniel hat Lust, ...	Anna findet es nett, ...

Tipp Grammatik – Wortschatz
Infinitiv mit *zu* steht
– nach bestimmten Verben (z. B. *versuchen, anfangen, helfen, vorhaben, ...*)
– nach bestimmten Verbkonstruktionen mit *haben* (z. B. *Zeit haben, Lust haben, ...*) und
– nach bestimmten Konstruktionen mit *es (es ist wichtig, es ist schön, ...)*.

B4 ▶ 172

9 Was wissen Sie noch? Lesen Sie die Sätze. Wo fehlt *zu* (___)? Ergänzen Sie. Hören Sie dann noch einmal und ergänzen Sie die Namen *Daniel* oder *Anna* (___).

a ______ möchte nächste Woche mit ______ in ein Konzert ___ gehen.
b ______ hat vor, am Donnerstag ihre Tante ___ besuchen.
c Am Mittwochnachmittag muss ______ zum Arzt ___ gehen.
d Am Mittwoch soll ______ Überstunden ___ machen.
e ______ versucht, für Mittwoch Konzertkarten ___ besorgen.
f ______ und ______ würden am Mittwoch lieber nicht ins Symphoniekonzert ___ gehen.

10 Verabredungen treffen. Ordnen Sie die Redemittel zu.

a ~~Ich würde gern mit dir ... gehen.~~ b Geht es am ... um ... Uhr? c Hast du Lust, am ... in ein Konzert / ins Kino / essen ... zu gehen? d Der ... passt leider nicht. Da habe ich vor, ... zu ... e Das ist gut, dann besorge/ reserviere/... ich ... f Am ... habe ich Zeit. g Tut mir leid, am ... kann ich nicht. Da muss ich ... h Hast du am ... Zeit? i Der ... passt gut. j Gut, dann treffen wir uns am ... um ...

jemanden einladen: a, ... absagen: den Termin vereinbaren:
einen Terminvorschlag machen: zusagen:

11 Sie möchten sich mit jemandem verabreden. Sie finden nicht sofort einen Termin. Ergänzen Sie und schreiben Sie einen Dialog mit den Redemitteln aus 10.

Sie möchten (Tennis spielen / ins Museum gehen / ...) ______.
Sie haben am ______ um ______ Uhr Zeit.
Ihre Partnerin / Ihr Partner hat am ______ um ______ Uhr keine Zeit.
Sie/Er muss ______.

○ Ich würde gern mit dir ... Geht es ...?
△ Tut mir leid, ...

C1 **1 Was wissen Sie noch? Lesen Sie noch einmal** → KB S. 138, C1a**. Wer sagt was? Ordnen Sie zu. Welche zwei Sätze passen nicht?**

tamina Figaro

a Figaro : Opernsänger bekommen an der Musikhochschule auch eine Fremdsprachenausbildung.
b ______ : Opernsänger geben manchmal Sprachunterricht.
c ______ : Es ist schwierig, Operntexte auswendig zu lernen.
d ______ : Opernsänger können den Inhalt ihrer Lieder verstehen, weil sie die Texte übersetzen können.
e ______ : Eine deutliche Aussprache ist für Opernsänger beim Sprachenlernen sehr wichtig.

C2 **2 Schreiben Sie die Wörter mit Artikel und ordnen Sie zu.**

1 2 3 4 5 6 7 8

9 10 11 12 ~~13~~ 14 15 16

a 13 das F e u _ _ z _ _ _
b ☐ ______ _ _ _ e i _ _ h o _ _
c ☐ ______ B _ h _ _
d ☐ ______ C r _ _ _
e ☐ ______ _ _ l z
f ☐ ______ _ _ _ _ _ u m _ _ _ l a g
g ☐ ______ _ _ _ p f
h ☐ ______ L i _ _ _
i ☐ ______ _ o _ _
j ☐ ______ T _ _ m
k ☐ ______ _ ü _ _ t o _ _ _
l ☐ ______ _ _ _ _ _ o l
m ☐ ______ T a _ _ _
n ☐ ______ _ _ _ f ü _
o ☐ ______ _ ü t _
p ☐ ______ _ _ o f _

3 Ellas „persönliche Sätze". Ergänzen Sie Wörter aus 2.

a Ich rauche nicht. Deshalb habe ich auch kein Feuerzeug. Auch (Pl.) ______ verwende ich selten.
b Der ______ ist meine Lieblingsschachfigur.
c Unser Sohn mag kein Gemüse. Er isst keine Karotten, keinen Salat und auch keine (Pl.) ______.
d Wir haben eine Stadtwohnung, aber ich würde gern in einem Haus aus ______ wohnen.
e Im Winter trage ich am liebsten warme, bunte Jacken mit großen (Pl.) ______.
f Ich finde es gut, dass es in unserem Supermarkt nur (Pl.) Papier______ gibt. Das ist besser für die Umwelt.
g Kosmetik ist nicht so wichtig für mich. Ich verwende eine Gesichts______, aber ich habe kein ______.

4 Was wissen Sie jetzt über Ella? Schreiben Sie.

a Ella raucht nicht. b Sie spielt ...

C3 **5 Was passt wo: *sehen, hören* oder *schmecken*? Ergänzen Sie.**

a ______
ein tolles Konzert
seine hohe Stimme
mein altes Klavier
welche kleine Flöte?
dieser windige Tag

b ______
das blaue Meer
ein interessanter Film
dieses kleine Mädchen mit dem hübschen Hut
diese roten Blumen auf deinem braunen Regal
welches neue Bild?

c ______
diese große Kanne mit dem heißen Tee
mein kleines Glas Milch
unsere süße Schokolade
seine große Portion Nudeln
reife Äpfel

6 Ordnen Sie die Artikel, Adjektive und Nomen aus 5 den Regeln zu.

Regeln	Beispiele
Hauptregel (HR): meistens -en	diese roten Blumen, ...
Singularegel 1 (SR1): nach • der, • das, • die, eine -e	das blaue Meer, ...
Singularregel 2 (SR2): nach ein • -er, • -es	ein tolles Konzert, ...
Pluralregel 1 (PL1): • „Nullartikel“ (ohne Artikel) im Nom. + Akk. -e	reife Äpfel, ...

Tipp Grammatik
Nach DER-Wörtern, z. B. *dieser, mancher, welcher, jeder, ...* (vgl. Lektion 15) stehen dieselben Adjektivendungen wie nach definitem Artikel *der, das, die.*

Nach EIN-Wörtern, z. B. *kein, mein, dein, sein, ihr, unser, euer* stehen dieselben Adjektivendungen wie nach indefinitem Artikel *ein, eine.*

7 Gegensätze. Was passt? Ergänzen Sie und ordnen Sie zu.

a Euch gefällt eure klein_e_ Stadtwohnung. 5
b Irene mag ihre dick______ Katze. ☐
c Margit und Bernd laden ihre nett______ Nachbarn gern ein. ☐
d Ich mag meinen alt______, langsam______ Computer. ☐
e Jeder neu______ Tag bringt neu______ Chancen. ☐

1 Andreas liebt seine bunt______ Fische.
2 Richard streitet ständig mit seinem unfreundlich______ Nachbarn.
3 Du liebst dein neu______, schnell______ • Notebook.
4 Jede zu kurz______ Nacht macht den Tag danach sehr anstrengend.
~~5~~ Wir mögen unser klein______ Haus mit Garten.

8 Lesen Sie den Text. Ergänzen Sie und ordnen Sie zu.

~~meinen wichtig en Termin~~ meinem klein____ Schreibtisch einem lang____ Arbeitstag
meine fröhlich____ Nachbarn meine schwierig____ Lernwörter ihre laut____ Kinder
mein schmutzig____ Geschirr ihren neu____ Instrumenten

Ich denke an ______________________ (a) in der Küche,
und an _meinen wichtigen Termin_ (b) morgen im Büro.
Ich höre ______________________ (c) Feste feiern
und ______________________ (d) auf ______________________ (e) spielen.
Deshalb kann ich mich so schlecht auf ______________________ (f) konzentrieren,
wenn ich endlich nach ______________________ (g)
an ______________________ (h) sitze
und versuche, Deutsch zu lernen.

Aussprache

▶ 173 **1** Hören Sie /r/, /l/ oder /n/? Kreuzen Sie an.

	/r/	/l/	/n/		/r/	/l/	/n/		/r/	/l/	/n/
a	☐	X	☐	e	☐	☐	☐	i	☐	☐	☐
b	☐	☐	☐	f	☐	☐	☐	j	☐	☐	☐
c	☐	☐	☐	g	☐	☐	☐	k	☐	☐	☐
d	☐	☐	☐	h	☐	☐	☐	l	☐	☐	☐

▶ 174 **2** Hören Sie und ergänzen Sie *r*, *l* oder *n*.

_r_eich – __eicht
er__eben – __eben
fa__ __en – fah__en

ste__ __en – ne__ __en
feh__en – Fe__ster
Zah__ – Zah__

Sa__z – Sa__d
__ass – __assen
füh__en – füh__en

▶ 175 **3** Hören Sie noch einmal und sprechen Sie nach.

Tipp Aussprache
Sprechen Sie „nnnnnn“. Halten Sie jetzt Ihre Nase zu: Aus „nnnnnn“ wird „llllll“. Zu /r/ vgl. Lektion 16.

Schreibwerkstatt

1 **Lesen Sie die E-Mail und beantworten Sie die Fragen.**

a Wozu will Gerda Anton und Luise einladen?

b Wann beginnt die Veranstaltung?

Hallo Luise, hallo Anton,

wart Ihr schon einmal in der Oper? Interessiert Ihr Euch dafür? Ich habe Opernkarten bekommen und wollte Euch fragen, ob Ihr mitgehen wollt. Die Karten sind für den 10.11., das ist ein Donnerstag. Die Oper beginnt um 19:30 Uhr.

Liebe Grüße
Gerda

2 **Wer sagt zu, wer sagt ab? Lesen Sie die Antworten und ergänzen Sie die Tabelle.**

Liebe Gerda,

vielen Dank für Deine Einladung. Leider kann ich am Donnerstagabend nicht mitgehen, weil Alex und ich Freunde zum Abendessen eingeladen haben. Alex und ich gehen regelmäßig in die Oper. Es gefällt uns immer sehr gut. Es macht Spaß, sich schön anzuziehen und dann drei Stunden lang wunderbare Musik zu hören. Vielleicht klappt es ja das nächste Mal. Ich wünsche Dir einen schönen Opernabend. Es wird sicher toll.

Herzliche Grüße
Luise

Liebe Gerda,

es freut mich sehr, dass Du an mich gedacht hast. Ich komme gern mit. Normalerweise habe ich am Donnerstag meinen Französischkurs, aber die Lehrerin ist krank und die Sprachenschule hat die Stunde abgesagt. Das heißt, ich habe Zeit mitzukommen. Wenn ich ehrlich bin, war ich noch nie in der Oper. Ich höre eigentlich nur Rock und Pop. Aber vielleicht ist es wichtig, auch einmal andere Musikrichtungen kennenzulernen. Was zieht man für die Oper an? Wie lange dauert es? Und wie viel kosten die Karten?
Ich bin auf jeden Fall um 19:15 Uhr vor der Oper. Ich freue mich.

Bis Donnerstag
Anton

	Absage	Zusage
Wer?		
Warum?		
Erfahrung mit Opernbesuchen		

3 **Lesen Sie die Situationen. Wählen Sie eine Situation aus und schreiben Sie eine Zu- oder Absage. Schreiben Sie zu jedem Punkt einige Sätze. Sie können auch eine eigene Einladung schreiben.**

a Ein Freund möchte mit Ihnen am Freitag ins Kino gehen. Er möchte einen Horrorfilm („Schwarz wie die Nacht") sehen. Der Film beginnt um 17:00 Uhr.

b Freunde laden Sie ein, mit Ihnen eine Kunstausstellung im Stadtmuseum zu besuchen. Die Ausstellung zeigt Kunst zwischen 1910 und 1950, vor allem Bilder von Otto Dix und Max Beckmann.

Zusage	Absage
Dank – Warum sagen Sie zu?	Dank – Warum sagen Sie ab?
Erfahrungen mit ähnlichen Veranstaltungen	Erfahrungen mit ähnlichen Veranstaltungen
Fragen (Dauer der Veranstaltung, Preis, ...)	Vorschläge für eine andere Veranstaltung

Vielen Dank für ... Ich habe mich sehr darüber gefreut.
Leider kann ich nicht ... mitkommen. Ich muss ...
Ich komme gern mit.
Ich finde ... toll/... ... gefällt mir nicht.

Ich bin/habe schon oft ...
Es ist immer wieder toll/interessant/..., zu ...
Wann treffen wir uns ...? Wie viel kosten ...?
Vielleicht hast du Lust, ... zu ...

→ Hier können Sie weiterlernen: www.hueber.de/motive

Lernwortschatz

Einstiegsseite
die Süßigkeit, -en

vorsichtig

gesund bleiben
Sport treiben

A1
der Ärger
die Autotür, -en
das Benzin
der Diesel
das Fahrzeug, -e
der Fußgänger, -
die Hauptstadt, ¨-e
die Panne, -n
der Radweg/ Fahrradweg, -e
der Stadtplan, ¨-e
die Tankstelle, -n
die Werkstatt, ¨-en
CH: die Garage, -n
das Zeichen, -

abbiegen
aussteigen
beeilen (sich)
bemerken
bremsen
herausfinden
kontrollieren
kommunizieren
parken
CH: parkieren
passen
stehen bleiben
steigen
tanken
verlieren
verpassen
A: versäumen
weiterfahren

dringend
plötzlich

hinterher
noch mal / noch einmal
per
per Autostopp
solch-
vorbei / vorbei-liegen lassen
Platz machen

A2
die Aufforde-rung, -en
die Autopapiere (Pl.)
der Kasten, ¨-
der Erste-Hilfe-Kasten, ¨-

aufschreiben
leihen
volltanken

A3
der Zettel, -

wegnehmen

betrunken

B1
die Apotheke, -n
der Fahrradunfall, ¨-e
das Mountainbike, -s
das Rezept, -e

bluten
herausfahren

mitten

etwas gegen
in den Bergen

B2
das Fieber-thermometer, -
die Grippe, -n
das Herz, -en
das Herzproblem, -e
der Husten
der Hustensaft, ¨-e
das Kleingeld
die Krankenkasse, -n
der Magen, ¨-
die Magen-schmerzen (Pl.)
das Mittel, -
die Quittung, -en
der Regenschirm, -e
der Schnupfen

einnehmen

schwanger

Medikamente einnehmen

B3
der Arztbesuch, -e
der Bikini, -s
die Puppe, -n
die Seife, -n
die Unter-suchung, -en

austeilen
einsammeln
untersuchen

notwendig

los sein

C1
die Bewegung, -en
die Droge, -n
der Geschwindig-keitsrekord, -e
die Küste, -n
die Ostküste
der Patient, -en
das Risiko, -s
der Spezialist, -en
die Tiefe
der Versuch, -e
die Westküste
das Wörterbuch, ¨-er

erreichen
stürzen
warnen

menschlich
neugierig
unvorsichtig

Ost-
während
West-

C2
der Rekord, -e
die Sportart, -en

extrem

C3
das Boot, -e
die Extrem-sportart, -en
die Folge, -n
die Forschung, -en
das U-Boot, -e

einsetzen (sich)
klettern
verbessern (sich)
verlassen
ziehen

anfangs
gegenseitig

einen Rekord aufstellen

A

A1 1 Was wissen Sie noch? Lesen Sie noch einmal → KB S. 142, A1a. Ergänzen Sie und ordnen Sie die Bilder zu.

a b c d e

Radfahrer unterwegs Tankstelle Fahrzeugs sich beeilen Zeichen
biegt ... ab Kreuzung ~~Autobahn~~ parkt Panne

Situation 1: e Ein Lastwagen fährt hinter Ihnen auf der Autobahn und gibt Ihnen ______ mit der Lichthupe. Der Fahrer möchte, dass Sie schneller fahren.
Situation 2: ☐ An der Ampel fährt ein ______ an Ihrem Auto vorbei und ______ rechts ______. Dabei verliert er seine Tasche. Die Ampel zeigt Rot.
Situation 3: ☐ Sie haben einen Termin und müssen ______. Sie möchten gerade bei Grün über die ______ gehen, da spricht Sie ein Tourist an. Er ist in der Stadt ______ und will Sie nach dem Weg fragen.
Situation 4: ☐ Ihr Kollege nimmt Sie in seinem Auto mit. Unterwegs haben Sie eine ______. Ihr Kollege hat an der letzten ______ Diesel getankt. Sein Auto fährt aber mit Benzin.
Situation 5: ☐ Sie sind auf einem Radweg unterwegs. Neben dem Radweg ______ ein Auto. Plötzlich öffnet der Fahrer des ______ die Autotür.

2 Lesen Sie verschiedene Antworten zu den Situationen in 1 und schreiben Sie die Wörter richtig. Welche Antworten passen zu welcher Beschreibung (A oder B)? Ordnen Sie zu.

A Sie behalten immer die Ruhe und kommen so auch mit schwierigen Situationen gut zurecht.

B Sie ärgern sich sehr oft im Straßenverkehr. Dabei bleiben Sie nicht immer höflich.

Situation 1: B Ich bleibe vor dem LKW und ~~sebrem~~ bremse. Ich denke: „Er soll sich ruhig ärgern."
Situation 2: ☐ Ich fahre dem **fahRadrer** ______ hinterher und gebe ihm die Tasche.
Situation 3: ☐ Ich bleibe stehen und zeige dem **gergänFuß** ______ den Weg auf dem Stadtplan.
Situation 4: ☐ Ich schimpfe und frage ihn, warum er nicht aufgepasst hat. Wir **senpasver** ______ jetzt unseren Termin.
Situation 5: ☐ Ich bin froh, dass ich noch einmal Glück gehabt habe und fahre einfach **terwei** ______.

A2 3 Welche Verkehrsmittel (____) passen zu welcher Situation (a–f)? Ordnen Sie zu. Ergänzen Sie dann *Wer? Wem?* oder *Was?* (~~~).

Auto Moped zu Fuß Flugzeug ~~Zug~~ Fahrrad

a Tina: Ich wollte wissen, wo ich umsteigen muss. ~Wer?~ Der Angestellte hat ~~~ mir ~~~ den Bahnhof und den Bahnsteig aufgeschrieben. (Zug)
b Emil und Anna: Wir wollten bei Regen die Altstadt besichtigen. ~~~ Der Rezeptionist hat ~~~ uns ~~~ einen Schirm geliehen. (______)
c Paula: ~~~ Ich habe ~~~ der Frau am Schalter ~~~ einen Koffer und eine Reisetasche gegeben. Man darf aber nur ein Gepäckstück einchecken. (______)
d Martin: Ich bin zwölf Jahre damit gefahren. Jetzt hat ~~~ mein Mechaniker ~~~ mir ~~~ ein Motorrad empfohlen. Das hat einen stärkeren Motor. (______)
e Frau Schuster: ~~~ Die Verkehrsregeln hat ~~~ Herr Lorenz ~~~ den Kindern sehr gut erklärt. Die Fahrradprüfung haben sie alle geschafft. (______)
f Jens: Auf der Heimfahrt hat man uns kontrolliert. ~~~ Manuel musste ~~~ der Polizistin ~~~ seinen Führerschein zeigen. (______)

4 Welche Personen aus 3 sind gemeint? Schreiben Sie Sätze und markieren Sie den Akkusativ (___) und Dativ (___) wie im Beispiel.

a Er musste ihn ihr zeigen. Manuel musste der Polizistin seinen Führerschein zeigen.
b Er hat sie mir aufgeschrieben. ____________
c Er hat es mir empfohlen. ____________
d Er hat sie ihnen sehr gut erklärt. ____________
e Ich habe sie ihr gegeben. ____________
f Er hat ihn uns geliehen. ____________

5 Ergänzen Sie die Verben. Markieren Sie dann den Akkusativ (___) und Dativ (___) wie im Beispiel.

geliehen erzählt kaufen zeige ~~schenken~~ geschickt geschrieben bringen zurückgebracht erklären hole

a ● Sollen wir Katrin zum Geburtstag ein Fahrrad schenken?
■ Ich wollte ihr ein Computerspiel ____________, aber ein Fahrrad ist sicher besser.

b ● Woher weißt du von Martinas Unfall?
■ Anuk hat mir die Geschichte ____________.

c ● Hast du Elisabeth dein Moped ____________?
■ Ja, aber sie hat es mir schon wieder ____________.

d ● Ich verstehe das nicht. Kannst du mir die Matheaufgabe ____________?
■ Ich ____________ dir eine gute Internetseite, die hilft dir sicher weiter.

e ● Alex, kannst du mir bitte mein Werkzeug ____________?
■ Ja, ich ____________ es dir sofort.

f ● Von wem ist dieser Brief? Hat dir jemand etwas Nettes ____________?
■ Nein, im Gegenteil. Die Werkstatt hat mir die Rechnung für die Reparatur ____________.

> **Tipp Grammatik**
> Bei Verben mit der Bedeutung *geben* oder *nehmen* (z. B. *schenken, holen, kaufen, …*) und bei Verben mit der Bedeutung *sagen* (z. B. *erzählen, erklären, …*) stehen sehr oft ein Dativ und ein Akkusativ. Der Dativ steht dann für die Person, der Akkusativ steht für eine Sache.
> Zum Beispiel: Ich schenke meiner Schwester eine CD.
> Einige Verben brauchen nur den Dativ (vgl. Lektion 8). Eine Liste der Verben mit Dativ finden Sie hier: www.hueber.de/motive

6 Ergänzen Sie die Pronomen.

Akkusativ	mich		ihn	sie	es		euch	
Dativ		dir			ihm	uns		ihnen/Ihnen

7 Ergänzen Sie die Pronomen im Akkusativ und im Dativ.

a ● Hier ist der Stadtplan für Lisa. Bringst du ihn ihr?
■ Klar, mache ich.

b ● Ich glaube, Herr Schön hat seine Autopapiere liegen lassen.
■ Kein Problem, ich bringe ______ ______ vorbei.

c ● Kannst du mir die Telefonnummer deiner Werkstatt geben?
■ Ja, einen Moment, ich gebe ______ ______ sofort.

d ● Habt ihr die Verkehrsregeln verstanden?
■ Ja, der Fahrlehrer hat ______ ______ gut erklärt.

e ● Könnte ich mein Handy wiederhaben?
■ Ich gebe ______ ______ sofort zurück. Ich muss nur noch Helga anrufen.

f ● Ich hoffe, ich habe meine Autoschlüssel nicht verloren.
■ Nein, sie liegen auf dem Schreibtisch, Herr Neuhold. Ich hole ______ ______ sofort.

8 Sagen Sie es höflicher. Schreiben Sie Sätze mit Konjunktiv wie im Beispiel.

a Dort liegt der Stadtplan für Jan. Gib ihn ihm, bitte!
b Hier ist die Rechnung für Johanna. Bezahl sie ihr, bitte!
c Der Hund hat mein Handy. Nimm es ihm bitte weg!
d Petra hat den Brief vom Amt noch gar nicht bemerkt. Zeig ihn ihr, bitte!
e Wie ist der Name des Films? Schreib ihn mir bitte auf! Ich will ihn nicht verpassen.

a Könntest du Jan bitte den Stadtplan geben? b …

B

B1 **1 Was wissen Sie noch? Hören Sie noch einmal. Was ist falsch? Korrigieren Sie die Fehler.**

▶ 176

Peter Krüger hatte einen Unfall mit dem Fahrrad. Der Unfall ist ~~auf dem Land~~ *im Stadtzentrum* passiert. Peter Krüger ist auf der Straße gefahren. Neben ihm haben mehrere Mopeds geparkt. Plötzlich ist eines aus dem Parkplatz herausgefahren. Peter Krüger konnte noch bremsen, er ist aber trotzdem hingefallen. Seine Hand hat geblutet, aber er musste nicht ins Krankenhaus. Er ärgert sich, dass der Autofahrer sich nicht konzentriert hat, und einfach weitergefahren ist. Peter Krüger meint, dass es mehr Autobusse und Straßenbahnen in der Stadt geben sollte.

Karin Fuchs hatte auch einen Autounfall. Peter Krüger will wissen, ob der Unfall mit einem Auto, einem Motorrad, einem Bus oder einer Straßenbahn passiert ist. Denn er glaubt, dass ihr Unfall auch auf dem Land passiert ist. Karin erzählt ihm, dass sie mit ihrem Mountainbike in den Bergen gegen einen Baum gefahren ist und sich am Bein verletzt hat. Sie war nicht im Krankenhaus, und sie hat immer noch Schmerzen. Deshalb hat sie ein Rezept bekommen. Jetzt holt sie das Medikament bei ihrem Arzt.

2 Ergänzen Sie die Indefinitpronomen.

	Nominativ	Akkusativ
Singular	● Da kommt ein Bus. ■ Und da kommt noch *einer*. ● Da kommt ein Taxi. ■ Und da kommt noch ________. ● Da kommt eine Straßenbahn. ■ Und da kommt noch ________.	● Da fährt kein Bus. ■ Doch, ich sehe ________. ● Da kommt kein Taxi. ■ Doch, ich sehe ________. ● Da fährt keine Straßenbahn. ■ Doch, ich sehe ________.
Plural	● Da kommen Fahrräder. ■ Ja, und dort kommen noch ________.	● Da gibt es keine Fahrräder. ■ Doch, ich sehe ________.

B2 **3 Was passt? Ergänzen Sie die richtigen Nomen (____) und Indefinitpronomen (~~~~).**

einen Erste-Hilfe-Kasten   ein Taxi   Radwege   eine Apotheke   einen Unfall   ~~ein Medikament~~

a ● Ich habe starke Kopfschmerzen. Hast du *ein Medikament*?
■ Ja, im Badezimmerschrank findest du sicher *ein(e)s*.

b ● Ich fahre gern Rad in der Stadt. Gibt es hier ____________?
■ Ja, am Fluss gibt es ~~~~.

c ● Vom Flughafen ins Stadtzentrum sind es 25 Kilometer. Nehmen wir doch ____________.
■ Ja, das machen wir. Schau, dort drüben steht ~~~~.

d ● Ich habe hier ein Rezept. Gibt es ____________ in der Nähe?
■ Ja, gegenüber dem Kino ist ~~~~.

e ● Jakob hatte vor einem Monat ____________ mit dem Fahrrad.
■ Ich hatte letzte Woche auch ~~~~.

f ● Guten Tag, ich brauche ____________ für mein Auto.
■ Gern, hier ist ~~~~. Er ist sehr günstig.

4 Ordnen Sie zu.

am Bein verletzt sein ~~sich mit dem Messer schneiden~~ ein Rezept bekommen Schmerzen im Arm haben hinfallen ~~den Notarzt rufen~~ Magenschmerzen haben Grippe bekommen Schnupfen bekommen ein Mittel gegen Kopfschmerzen nehmen ~~40 Grad Fieber haben~~ Zahnschmerzen haben Husten haben einen Unfall haben Hustensaft kaufen Herzprobleme haben Tabletten nehmen Tee trinken sich verletzen

krank werden	krank sein	Hilfe bekommen / gesund werden
sich mit dem Messer schneiden	40 Grad Fieber haben	den Notarzt rufen

5 Ergänzen Sie Wörter aus 4.

krank werden

a Der Boden ist nass. Pass auf, dass du nicht hinfällst.
b In unserem Büro sind schon fast alle krank. Ich hoffe, ich bekomme nicht auch die ______.
c Du musst aufpassen, beim Mountainbiken kann man sich leicht ______.

krank sein

d Ich glaube, ich habe eine Grippe. Ich habe Kopfschmerzen und 40 Grad ______.
e Er ist ______. Er kann nicht Fußball spielen.
f Ich brauche einen Termin beim Zahnarzt. Ich habe ______.

Hilfe bekommen / gesund werden

g Ich habe von meinem Arzt ______ bekommen. Ich muss zur Apotheke, die Medikamente holen.
h Sie haben Husten und Schnupfen. Trinken Sie ______ und kaufen Sie einen guten ______.
i Da vorne ist ein Unfall passiert. Hat jemand ______?

▶ 177–183 **6** Hören Sie die Situationen (a–g). Welche Überschrift passt zu welcher Situation? Ordnen Sie zu.

1 Zahnschmerzen 2 Husten 3 Baby 4 Quittung 5 Kopfschmerzen 6 ~~Schnupfen~~ 7 Tierarzt

a 6 b ___ c ___ d ___ e ___ f ___ g ___

▶ 177–183 **7** Hören Sie noch einmal. Was ist gemeint? Schreiben Sie die Nomen zu den unterstrichenen Pronomen.

a … Ich glaube, <u>meine</u> sind besser. Mein Schnupfen ist weg. meine Medikamente
b … <u>Eure</u> ist so oft krank. <u>Unsere</u> musste noch nie zum Arzt. ______
c … Ja, ich kann dir <u>meinen</u> empfehlen. ______
d … Ich glaube, ich habe <u>welche</u> in meiner Handtasche. ______
e … Richard hat letzte Woche auch <u>einen</u> gekauft. Ich glaube, <u>seiner</u> war viel billiger. ______
f … Moment. Hier ist <u>eine</u>. ______
g … Und ich dachte, sie hat schon <u>eins</u>. ______

8 Ein Tag im Krankenhaus. Ergänzen Sie.

a • Aber ich wollte keinen Schinken, das ist nicht mein Frühstück.
▪ Stimmt, das ist meines. Ihres kommt noch.
b • Ich muss noch meine Medikamente nehmen.
▪ Warten Sie, das sind meine Tabletten. ______ haben Sie schon eingenommen.
c • Der Morgenmantel ist ein bisschen eng.
▪ Das ist mein Mantel. ______ hängt im Schrank.
d • Jetzt habe ich Appetit auf meine Nachspeise.
▪ Das ist meine Orange, ______ haben Sie schon zu Mittag gegessen.
e • Der Tee ist viel zu heiß.
▪ Das ist mein Tee. ______ muss die Schwester noch bringen.
f • Könnten Sie das Licht ausschalten? Ich möchte schlafen.
▪ Meines habe ich ausgeschaltet. ______ ist noch an.

C

C1 **1 Was wissen Sie noch? Lesen Sie noch einmal** → KB S. 146, C1a**. Was ist richtig? Kreuzen Sie an.**

a Viele Ärzte empfehlen
- ☐ nicht zu viel Bewegung zu machen.
- ☐ täglich mit dem Rad zu fahren.
- ☐ sich im Fitnessstudio fit zu halten.

b Beim „Race Across America" müssen die Teilnehmer
- ☐ von der Westküste zur Ostküste der USA fahren.
- ☐ 5000 km in einer Woche fahren.
- ☐ während der Fahrt Pausen machen.

c Die Schweizerin Trix Zgraggen
- ☐ hat beim „Race Across America" mitgemacht.
- ☐ war schneller als alle anderen Teilnehmer.
- ☐ ist täglich mit dem Rad zur Arbeit gefahren.

d Markus Stöckl
- ☐ ist bei einem Rekordversuch gestürzt.
- ☐ erreicht bei seinen Rekordversuchen mehr als 200 km/h.
- ☐ ist bei seinen Rekordversuchen oft unvorsichtig.

e Psychologen warnen davor,
- ☐ dass Sport zu einer Droge wird.
- ☐ dass Hobbysportler an ihre Grenzen gehen.
- ☐ dass Sportler nicht neugierig genug sind.

C2 **2 Nomen mit *-er*, *-in* oder *-ung*. Schreiben Sie die Verben zu den Nomen.**

a der Schwimmer, die Schwimmerin: schwimmen
b die Empfehlung: ______
c die Vorbereitung: ______
d die Untersuchung: ______
e der Fußballspieler, die Fußballspielerin: Fußball ______
f der Arbeiter, die Arbeiterin: ______
g die Verletzung: ______
h der Anfänger, die Anfängerin: ______
i der Läufer, die Läuferin: ______
j die Erklärung: ______

3 Lesen Sie die Sätze und ergänzen Sie Nomen aus 2.

a Carina spielt noch nicht lange Volleyball, sie ist noch Anfängerin.
b Mountainbiken ist gefährlich, es kommt immer wieder zu ______ (Pl.).
c Wie funktioniert die Abseitsregel im Fußball? Ich habe die ______ noch nicht ganz verstanden.
d Nach seinem Unfall musste der Sportler sofort zur ______ ins Krankenhaus.
e Es war ein schwieriges Rennen für alle ______ und ______.
f Ich weiß nicht, welcher Sport für Sie passt. Da kann ich Ihnen leider keine ______ geben.

C3 **4 Ergänzen Sie wie in den Beispielen.**

	Fragewort	jemand	niemand
Nominativ			
Akkusativ	Wen?	jemanden	
Dativ			niemandem

a
- ● Ist da ~~~ (Wer?) jemand?
- ■ Nein, da ist ~~~ niemand.

b
- ● Hast du nicht mit ~~~ jemandem gesprochen?
- ■ Nein, ich habe ~~~ niemanden gesehen.

c
- ● Ich habe aber ~~~ jemanden gehört.
- ■ Ich nicht, und ich habe auch mit ~~~ niemandem gesprochen.

5 Ergänzen Sie die richtige Form von *jemand* oder *niemand*.

a
- ● Kennst du (Wen?) jemanden, der jeden Tag Sport treibt?
- ■ Nein, ich kenne (Wen?) ______.

b Ich würde gern mit (Wem?) ______ Tennis spielen. Hat (Wer?) ______ Lust?

c
- ● Wo ist der Tennisplatz?
- ■ Ich weiß nicht, fragen wir doch (Wen?) ______.

d Ihr habt eine Raftingtour gemacht? Warum hat mir das (Wer?) ______ gesagt? Ich wollte auch mitkommen.

e
- ● Kennst du Eric Barone?
- ■ Nein, ich glaube, den kennt (Wer?) ______ hier.

f
- ● Wart ihr Mountainbiken?
- ■ Ja, aber ich glaube, es hat (Wem?) ______ gefallen. Es war zu anstrengend.

6 Lesen Sie den Text schnell und ignorieren Sie die hell markierten (= unbekannten) Wörter. Beantworten Sie dann die Fragen.

a Was macht Jana Mittermeier in ihrer Freizeit? ____________________
b Welche Pläne hatten Janas Eltern für ihre Tochter? ____________________
c Was ist Janas Freund Alex passiert? ____________________
d Was ist Janas Ziel? ____________________

Janas Traum

Ihre Freundinnen verbringen die Freizeit mit der Familie oder gehen mit Freunden ins Kino. Jana Mittermeier ist jeden Tag stundenlang in den Bergen unterwegs. Tägliches Training ist die Voraussetzung (a) für die schwierigen Expeditionen (b), die Jana in den nächsten Jahren vorhat. Jana liebt das Bergsteigen (c). Ihre Eltern können das nicht verstehen. Sie würden ihre Tochter lieber in einem „normalen" Beruf sehen. Eigentlich sollte Jana die Matura machen und dann mit einem Studium beginnen. Doch sie hat sich schon mit fünfzehn eher für waghalsige (d) Bergtouren als für dicke Schulbücher interessiert. Gegen den Willen (e) der Eltern hat sie die Schule abgebrochen (f) und sich nur noch auf das Bergsteigen konzentriert. Ihre erste große Expedition hat sie gemeinsam mit ihrem Freund Alex unternommen, auch er ein begeisterter (g) Bergsteiger. Doch vor zwei Jahren ist Alex tödlich verunglückt (h). Er war auf dem Traunstein, ihrem Hausberg (i), unterwegs. Ein unerwarteter (j) Wetterumschwung (k) hat den Abstieg (l) ins Tal fast unmöglich gemacht. Alex sah, wie ein anderer Kletterer in Bergnot (m) kam, und wollte ihm helfen. Dabei stürzte er in die Tiefe.

Danach hat Jana ein halbes Jahr lang keinen Berg bestiegen. Doch dann begann sie wieder mit dem Training. „Da bin ich Alex am nächsten", meint sie. Ihr nächstes großes Ziel ist der Cho Oyu an der Grenze zwischen China und Nepal. Es wäre ihr erster Achttausender (n).

7 Versuchen Sie, die Bedeutung der hell markierten Wörter zu verstehen. Welche Wortart sind die Wörter? Ordnen Sie die Erklärungen zu und übersetzen Sie die Wörter in Ihre Muttersprache.

auf Berge steigen, klettern · sehr gefährlich · ~~was notwendig ist~~ · sehr interessiert sein · wenn man hinunter steigt · Berg neben dem Heimatort · bei einem Unfall sterben · nicht erwartet · Berg, der mehr als 8000 m hoch ist · wenn das Wetter plötzlich anders wird · eine anstrengende, schwierige Reise · aufhören · was jemand will · Probleme beim Klettern haben

Wort	Wortart	Erklärung	Übersetzung
a Voraussetzung	Nomen	was notwendig ist	

Aussprache

▶ 184 **1** Hören Sie. Wann hören Sie /h/ am Wortanfang? Kreuzen Sie an.

	/h/	kein /h/
a	X	☐
b	☐	☐
c	☐	☐
d	☐	☐
e	☐	☐
f	☐	☐
g	☐	☐
h	☐	☐
i	☐	☐
j	☐	☐

▶ 185 **2** Hören Sie und sprechen Sie nach.

haben – aber · Eis – heiß · Husten – unten · hören – Ohren · offen – hoffen · er – Herr · hier – ihr · hinterher – immer mehr

▶ 186 **3** Lesen Sie die Sätze. Was sagt die Ärztin (= Ä)? Was sagt der Patient (= P)? Ordnen Sie zu. Hören Sie dann und sprechen Sie nach.

a [P] Ich habe Husten und Halsschmerzen.
b ☐ Wie lange haben Sie schon Halsschmerzen?
c ☐ Gegen den Husten hilft ein heißer Tee.
d ☐ Haben Sie hier Schmerzen?
e ☐ Sie müssen den Hustensaft noch heute holen.
f ☐ Ich hatte heute zu Hause Herzschmerzen.

SCHREIBWERKSTATT

1 Lesen Sie die beiden E-Mails. Wer schreibt Ihnen beruflich (= B), wer privat (= P)? Ordnen Sie zu.

A ☐

Hallo ...,

es hat geklappt. Ich habe meine zwei Urlaubswochen bekommen! Das heißt, wir sehen uns in ein paar Tagen. Ich freue mich darauf, Dich wiederzusehen. Es ist schon lange her, dass Du mich in Deutschland besucht hast. Ich bin jetzt dabei, meine Reise vorzubereiten. Wie ist eigentlich das Wetter bei Euch? Was soll ich einpacken? Sind T-Shirts und Jeans o. k. oder brauche ich auch warme Sachen? Spielst Du eigentlich Tennis? Ich könnte meine Tennissachen einpacken. Du hast geschrieben, dass Du auch frei hast, und wir in den zwei Wochen etwas zusammen unternehmen. Weißt Du schon, was wir machen? Ich bin so neugierig auf Dein Heimatland und Deine Heimatstadt. Wie sieht es bei euch aus? Welche typischen Speisen und Getränke gibt es? Was macht man in der Freizeit? Du siehst, ich will schon vorher alles wissen. ;-)

Bitte schreib mir bald
Gerlinde

B ☐

Sehr geehrte ...,

... das Treffen in Ihrer Firma kann leider nicht am nächsten Dienstag stattfinden. Herr Krüger, der Mitarbeiter, der an dem Treffen teilnehmen soll, ist noch bis Mittwoch auf einer Geschäftsreise. Er könnte aber am Donnerstag zu Ihnen kommen. Können Sie uns bitte sagen, ob Donnerstag als Termin für Sie passt? Herr Krüger würde das Flugzeug nehmen. Es gibt einen Flug am Morgen. Die Ankunftszeit ist 10:00 Uhr. Können Sie Herrn Krüger vom Flughafen abholen oder soll er ein Taxi nehmen? Könnten Sie ein Hotelzimmer für unseren Mitarbeiter reservieren? Herr Krüger möchte auch das Wochenende in Ihrer Stadt verbringen, er braucht also ein Zimmer für vier Tage. Vielen Dank für Ihre Hilfe.

Mit freundlichen Grüßen
Walter Kuhn

P. S.: Könnten Sie Herrn Krüger auch ein paar Tipps für das Wochenende geben?

2 Lesen Sie noch einmal. Was möchten die Personen wissen? Unterstreichen Sie die Fragen in den E-Mails.

3 Schreiben Sie zu einer der E-Mails eine Antwort.

Hallo / Liebe ...
Ich freue mich, dass Du ...
Du fragst mich, wie / was / wo / wohin ...
Das Wetter ist im Frühling / Mai / ... gut / nicht so gut.
Es regnet / schneit ... | Die Sonne ... | Es gibt Nebel / ...
Du solltest also ... einpacken.
Ich spiele / spiele nicht ... | Du könntest also / aber ...
Ich habe mir gedacht, dass wir ... könnten.
Du willst auch wissen, ob / wie / was ...
Mein Heimatland / Meine Heimatstadt ist ... | Es gibt ...
Man isst / trinkt gern ... Wir ... gern ...
Ich zeige Dir gern ...
Ich freue mich auf Dich.
Bis bald ...

Sehr geehrter Herr ...,
vielen Dank für die Nachricht / die Information.
Donnerstag passt / passt leider nicht.
Wir könnten den Termin auf ... verschieben.
Vielleicht können Sie / kann Herr Krüger ...
Ich kann ... gern abholen / leider nicht abholen.
Herr Krüger kann ein Taxi / den Bus / ... nehmen.
Die Fahrt dauert ... | Ich kann das Hotel ... empfehlen.
Ich reserviere gern ...
Ich schicke Ihnen die Reservierung / Informationen über ...
Ich kann ... gern Tipps geben. | Bei uns kann man ...
Es gibt ... | Touristen besichtigen gern ...
Vielleicht hat Herr Krüger Lust, ... Dann könnte er ...
Bitte teilen Sie uns mit, ob ... für Sie passt.
Mit freundlichen Grüßen
...

→ Hier können Sie weiterlernen: www.hueber.de/motive

Quellenverzeichnis

Titelbild: © Getty Images/fStop/Martin Diebel
S. 71: © Thinkstock/Wavebreak Media
S. 77: A © Thinkstock/iStock/Tashi-Delek;
B © Thinkstock/iStock/starush
S. 79: oben: © iStock/nullplus;
unten: © Thinkstock/iStock/97
S. 85: © Colourbox/Anja Robanke
S. 86: © Thinkstock/iStock/Dean Mitchell
S. 93: Wettersymbole © fotolia/Bastetamon
S. 94: oben: © Thinkstock/iStock/tekinturkdogan;
Mitte: © Thinkstock/iStock/Mark Bowden;
unten: © Thinkstock/iStock/Sura Nualpradid
S. 100: a © Thinkstock/iStock/Mark Poprocki;
b, d, k © Thinkstock/iStock/matheesaengkaew;
c © Thinkstock/iStock/Korovin;
e © Thinkstock/iStock/Alexander Yurkinskiy;
f © Thinkstock/iStock/Yordan Markov;
g © Thinkstock/Photodisc;
h © Thinkstock/iStock/Jillwt;
i © Thinkstock/iStock/Levent Konuk;
j © Thinkstock/iStock/mamadela;
Tafel © Thinkstock/iStock/Oliver Hoffmann;
unten von links: © iStock/delectus, © Thinkstock/iStock/Arne Trautmann, © fotolia/vbaleha
S. 101: unten von links: © Thinkstock/Pixland, © Thinkstock/iStock/Berc, © Thinkstock/iStock/Artush,
© Thinkstock/iStock/Alexander Yakovlev
S. 104: Spaghetti © Thinkstock/iStock/Magone;
Sandwich © Thinkstock/Monkey Business Images
S. 110: oben: © Thinkstock/iStock/pojoslaw;
unten: © Thinkstock/iStock/JackF
S. 111: 1 © Thinkstock/iStock/Alexander Raths;
2 © Thinkstock/iStock/Remains;
3 © Thinkstock/iStock/Dean Mitchell;
4 © Thinkstock/Photodisc;
5 © Thinkstock/iStock/istockphotoluis;
6 © Thinkstock/iStock/Jacob Wackerhausen
S. 112: von oben links: © Thinkstock/iStock/Dean Mitchell,
© Thinkstock/iStock/shironosov,
© Thinkstock/iStock/skifserg,
© Thinkstock/iStock/monkeybusinessimages,
© Thinkstock/Fuse, © Thinkstock/iStock/lisafx,
© Thinkstock/Wavebreak Media
S. 119: oben: Kamera © Thinkstock/iStock/Bet_Noire,
altes Foto © Thinkstock/iStock/mikhail pogosov;
unten: © Thinkstock/iStock/monkeybusinessimages
S. 120: oben: © Thinkstock/Hemera;
unten: © Thinkstock/iStock/Ekaterina Krasnikova
S. 122: 1 © Thinkstock/Polka Dot/Jupiter Images;
2 © Thinkstock/iStockphoto
S. 124: Reisetasche © iStockphoto/maureenpr;
Handgepäck © Thinkstock/iStockphoto;
Koffer © Thinkstock/iStock/Alexander Shirokov
S. 128: oben: © Neuhaus, www.erockit-bike.com;
unten: © Peel Engineering
S. 130: 3 Fotos: Wilfried Krenn, Graz
S. 132: Hund © Thinkstock/iStock/damedeeso;
Bushaltestelle © Thinkstock/iStock/krivinis; streitende Kollegen © Thinkstock/iStock/BartekSzewczyk; Mann © Thinkstock/iStock/innovatedcaptures; Arbeitsunfall © Thinkstock/iStock/pojoslaw
S. 145: © fotolia/VRD

Zeichnungen: Mascha Greune, München